Tunbridge Wells
A Second Selection
IN OLD PHOTOGRAPHS

Following her laying of the foundation stone of the Kent and Sussex Hospital on 19 July 1932 HRH the Duchess of York, later to become Queen Elizabeth the Queen Mother, accepts from Pauline Summers the first of two purses from the Peanuts Club representing a £400 contribution to the hospital appeal. Donations from numerous other quarters had by that time brought the appeal proceeds to £14,700. Later the Duchess dined at Bayham Abbey with the Marquis and Marchioness Camden and attended the annual agricultural show where she 'chatted freely, and in homely manner' with the accompanying civic guests and nobility.

Tunbridge Wells

A Second Selection

IN OLD PHOTOGRAPHS

M.L.J. ROWLANDS
and I.C. BEAVIS

Alan Sutton Publishing Limited
Phoenix Mill · Far Thrupp · Stroud
Gloucestershire

First Published 1994

Copyright © Tunbridge Wells Museum and Art
Gallery, 1994

Cover photograph: The Pantiles viewed from
Bath Square, *c.* 1860

British Library Cataloguing in Publication Data.
A catalogue record for this book is available from
the British Library.

ISBN 0–7509–0533–6

Typeset in 9/10 Sabon.
Typesetting and origination by
Alan Sutton Publishing Limited.
Printed in Great Britain by
Ebenezer Baylis, Worcester.

Contents

Piping the haggis at the Calverley Grounds in the early 1950s. A *Courier* photograph.

Introduction

These photographs from the Tunbridge Wells Museum collections are a further selection of views showing people, places, events, associations, and businesses in and around the town dating from the 1860s to a time shortly after local government reorganization in the 1970s. They are drawn from guidebooks, albums, scrapbooks, postcards, newspapers, and individual prints and snapshots by professionals and amateurs.

Despite their small size, some of the best photographs in this collection are taken from postcards. Over the century since picture postcards came into use, postcards have been manufactured using a wide range of techniques. Unlike the majority of photographic postcards produced via photolithography and photogravure, some manufacturers after the turn of this century turned to the superior, though labour-intensive, method of genuine photograph postcards. That is, rather than employing a printing process which invariably diminished the image quality, some professional photographers produced their own postcards which were actually mass-produced photographic prints. A column of editorial/advertisement explaining use of the new technique by Tunbridge Wells photographer Percy Lankester appeared in a June 1904 issue of the *Kent and Sussex Courier* newspaper:

We have in the past been accustomed to local views made in Germany, in which the Teutonic artist has bathed our scenery in an impossible atmosphere born of his own imagination, and the sylvan charm of the neighbourhood has been immersed in the same gaudy colouring which has been employed to illustrate a week in Lucerne, or a cheap trip up the Rhine. Latterly some English firms of note have given us a superior souvenir, and now we have a local atelier next this 'Courier' office, in which Picture Post Cards – which are really photographs – are turned out in any quantity, at the price per copy of a humble coin of the realm. The process of production adopted by Mr Percy Lankester is a very interesting one. Each card is printed from an actual negative by an ingenious process, which enables a large sheet, containing probably a score of views to be printed, as it were, with a single impression. For this purpose, a roll of sensitised paper, which is afterwards cut up to single Post Cards, is wound through a large chest, in which is a light screen, through which the rays of electric lamps pass through the negatives, and thence on to the cardboard. A few seconds' exposure to the concentrated artificial light, and the roll can be wound preparatory for the next set of impressions, and when the end of a roll is reached the usual processes of the dark room follow, and the sheets are hung to dry like a domestic array in a small laundry. Then the cards are cut up into single copies as they appear at Mr Lankester's studio and very artistic these views are, as some of the best negatives of picture photography, for which the Great Hall studio is famous, have been utilised in the process.

Since the resulting photographs, in postcard form, were usually produced from large-format negatives, the clarity and detail of the resulting cards could be astonishing compared to postcards printed using non-photographic processes.

A few photographs reproduced here are clearly of lesser quality than the postcards described above. These are views taken from photographs already reproduced in newspapers or guidebooks. Once already printed via the modern screen-printed halftone reproduction methods, further reproduction results in some loss of clarity since each reproduction requires screening of the 'original', each screening beyond the first usually resulting in so-called moiré type interference. Despite this risk, each of these pictures has been included since no original photographic print survives and since the unique historical picture content, an event or a place shown at a particular time, is not captured elsewhere. For example, to include a view of the Lord De L'Isle and Dudley's Boy Scouts collecting for the *Titanic* disaster Mansion House Fund in 1912 there is little alternative but to use the coarse photograph published at the time in the *Tunbridge Wells Advertiser* newspaper.

In many later instances the photographic prints of events survive, thus allowing better reproduction. For events of unusual importance, such as the visit of the Duchess of Kent in 1932, sometimes albums were compiled to record the occasion. Also, numerous prints survive of photographs by Press photographers who were covering newsworthy events for the newspapers. Some of the best topographical views are from albums compiled by professional photographers. George Glanville produced for sale albums of sepia prints of well-known Tunbridge Wells locations with descriptive captions, whereas D.J. Johnson's album features numerous obscure corners of the town which one often does not notice. Regardless of picture quality, from an historical viewpoint the best views in this, or any other, collection show places which by now have changed almost beyond recognition – such as Mount Pleasant in the 1860s and Tunbridge Wells Common before grazing ceased – or they show events in the town which are vaguely remembered or which no-one living could possibly remember – like the building of the Civic Centre and the world's first motor show.

SECTION ONE

People

The Nevill family of Eridge Park has played its part in Tunbridge Wells history from the beginning. In 1608 Lord Abergavenny sunk the first well over the chalybeate spring, discovered by Lord North while staying at Eridge. This group (*c.* 1862) shows standing at centre the 4th Earl of Abergavenny, Revd William Nevill (1792–1868), and on his left his son William (1826–1915), created 1st Marquess in 1876. The three children are (left to right) Henry (later 3rd Marquess), Reginald (later 2nd Marquess), and George (father of 4th Marquess).

The 4th Marquess of Abergavenny (1883–1954) with the Duchess of York at the Tunbridge Wells and South East Counties' Agricultural Show, of which he was patron, on 19 July 1932. The showground was off Eridge Road. The Duchess had come to Royal Tunbridge Wells to lay the foundation stone of the Kent and Sussex Hospital. She attended the show after lunch at Bayham Abbey with the Marquis and Marchioness Camden.

William Charles Cripps (1855–1952), a solicitor by profession, was appointed Clerk to the Local Board, the town's original local government, in 1887. When Tunbridge Wells became a borough in 1889, he became town clerk, serving until 1925. On retirement he was elected a freeman of the borough. In 1929 he became a member of Kent County Council, and in 1940 was elected a county alderman. On his death the *Courier* wrote that 'His name will always be associated with the history of Tunbridge Wells, for no one rendered it more eminent service, nor was there a man who was more respected'.

'In Fire Brigade circles the name of the Tunbridge Wells Brigade and its chief Captain Edward Westbrook are as familiar as household words', wrote the *Advertiser* in 1897, describing how under his leadership the town had developed 'for a place of its size, the best equipped fire service in the kingdom'. Westbrook (1853–1906), 'a gallant and energetic fireman', joined the brigade in 1875, and became captain in 1882. He was the father of Alderman Charles Westbrook, mayor in 1925–7 and 1938–45.

Robert Willsher Weekes, founder of the well-known department store at the foot of Mount Pleasant (taken over by Hoopers in 1990), opened his original shop in 1854. He was elected to the local board in 1884 and became a councillor when the town was incorporated in 1889. In 1892 he was elected an alderman, but died only three months later. He was succeeded in business by his son, Ernest Barten Weekes, who also served as a councillor and was mayor from 1934 to 1936.

Alderman Hori Pink (1836–1905), second mayor of Tunbridge Wells, served from 1891 to 1893. After his apprenticeship in the building and upholstering trade, he set up in business in Church Road, moving in 1869 to Grosvenor Road, with builder's workshops in St John's Road. 'He carried out some of the largest and best buildings in the town, especially in Bishops Down and Hungershall Park' (the *Advertiser*). Like many prominent tradesmen he became involved in local government, joining the local board in 1870 and being elected an alderman at the first meeting of the new town council.

'No one has done so much as the present mayor to infuse into the "sleepy hollow" of this most charming Kentish inland watering-place the life-blood of the latest scientific improvements' wrote a journalist in *The Sketch*. Sir David Lionel Salomons, 2nd Baronet (1851–1925), although not a councillor, consented to hold mayoral office in 1894–5. He was an enthusiastic engineer, a scientist and inventor, and a pioneer of electricity and motorized transport. 'His very ample fortune has permitted him to indulge in surrounding himself with examples of scientific instruments which, for variety and beauty of construction, are the finest extant.'

This lantern slide of *c.* 1900 shows Sir David's residence, Broomhill near Southborough, begun by his uncle, the 1st Baronet, in 1851. The water tower cum astronomical observatory behind was completed in 1876. Four years later work finished on a theatre (used for scientific demonstrations, and equipped in 1914 with the world's largest electric organ) and workshops to contain 60,000 electrically powered machine tools capable of producing 'almost any wooden or metal object that the heart of man can desire, or his head invent' (Hector Maclean).

Britain's first exhibition of motor vehicles was organized by David Salomons at the Agricultural Showground on 15 October 1895. This exhibit was built by Panhard and Levassor of Paris with a Daimler engine. Sir David, only the second Englishman to own a motor car, was founder (in 1896) of the Self-propelled Traffic Association (forerunner of today's RAC). He successfully campaigned against legal restrictions which effectively prevented cars being driven on public roads, and drew up technical clauses for the resultant new Act of 1896.

David Salomons' mayoral year was such a spectacular success that no one was willing to succeed him. Eventually Major Charles Robert Fletcher Lutwidge (1836–1907) was suggested. 'In vain he protested that he knew nothing of local administration. His hesitation had to yield to a numerously and influentially signed memorial' (the *Courier*). He served from 1895–8, was then elected an alderman, and was mayor again in 1901–2. Involved in numerous local organizations, he was a founder of the Volunteer Fire Brigade and the Salvage Corps.

Fletcher Lutwidge was succeeded as mayor by Alderman Frank William Stone (1841–1921), who served from 1898 to 1900. He was credited with 'saving the Commons' at a time when the Freeholders were accused of permitting too many encroachments such as the enclosure of St Helena Cottage. In 1883 he organized a takeover of the Freeholders by registering (not without resistance) himself and a group of like minded and eligible people. The newcomers secured a majority to elect a new committee to manage the Commons.

The famous contralto Clara Butt (1873–1935) performed at the Opera House on 9 April 1904 along with her husband, the baritone Robert Kennerley Rumford (1870–1957), whom she had married in 1900. They often appeared on stage together. She was later (1920) to be created a Dame of the British Empire for her performances in aid of charities during the First World War. This photograph of the couple was purchased as a souvenir of their visit to the town.

Colonel Edward Sydney St Barbe Sladen (1862–1921) was born in Upper Burma. He served twenty years with the Royal Montgomery Militia, and fought in Africa with the Ashanti Field Force in 1900. He came to Tunbridge Wells in 1907, was invited to become mayor in 1910 and re-elected in 1911. He continued on the council until 1915, and served again from 1917 to 1921. As mayor he organized the local celebrations of George V's coronation, 'carried out on a magnificent scale largely owing to his generosity' (the *Advertiser*).

Colonel Sladen lived at Rusthall Beacon (now the Beacon Hotel) and devoted much effort to landscaping and planting the extensive grounds (including Happy Valley). The house contained many artefacts brought from Burma by his father Sir Edward Sladen, including two golden umbrellas presented by King Mindon when he put down a rebellion. In the garden was Sir Edward's Burmese temple bell, which the colonel bequeathed to the council and which was erected in the rose garden in Calverley Grounds in 1935.

Sir Robert Vaughan Gower (1880–1953) joined the town council in 1909, was an alderman from 1915 until 1934 and mayor from 1917 to 1919. He served on Kent County Council from 1910 to 1926. In 1919 he was knighted for promoting a scheme for maintaining the businesses of tradesmen serving in the First World War. He was MP for Hackney from 1924, and for Gillingham from 1929 to 1945. Greatly interested in animal welfare, he was chairman of the RSPCA from 1928 and introduced legislation on preventing cruelty and on the protection of wild birds.

'Today Royal Tunbridge Wells is one of the most attractive inland resorts in Britain,' declared the 1955 guide. 'It retains much of its old-world charm, and visitors to the historic Pantiles may still enjoy the sparkling medicinal waters of the springs from which the town originated.' This contemporary photograph belongs to a collection assembled to illustrate official guides. The expression of disgust on the face of one of the girls taking the waters doubtless accounts for its not being used.

'To those whose years demand a somewhat stern view of life, it is always invigorating and refreshing to be in the company of happy careless children . . . and the cares which come upon one with life's maturity are oftimes banished for a little while under the infectious gaiety of childhood . . . Pattering feet kept in continuous movement by bright eyed lads and lasses whose costumes made a blaze of pretty colour; dreamy dance music, and an atmosphere of happiness – such in a nutshell, was the scene in the ball room. Surely it was a picture bright enough and jolly enough to make the hearts of the elders beat faster.' So the *Advertiser*'s enthusiastic reporter described the Juvenile Fancy Dress Ball given by the Mayor and Mayoress, Colonel and Mrs Sydney Sladen at the Spa Hotel on 4 January 1911, and attended by nearly 300 children. Here we see Master Jack Watson as 'Sailor Boy', Miss Joan Robinson as 'Pink Fairy', and Master Aubrey Milton Aubin as 'King of Cadonia'.

The *Courier*'s reporter was equally enraptured by the scene: 'The originality, costliness, splendour, and comprehensiveness of the costumes have certainly never been surpassed. . . . The natural shyness of the children quickly disappeared when the dancing began, and soon the room rang with the laughter and chatter of merry voices as partners were selected, not necessarily with a special eye to similarity in age or size; and as delighted couples tripped round in the leisurely waltz or scampered in the lively galop. Such a picture of perfect happiness and gay movement was a joy of itself. Meanwhile the tiny children who could not join in the fun of the ball-room . . . indulged in pretty little games, and clearly were not the least happy of the joyous throng'. This (Miss Gladys Semple, aged twelve, 'Japanese Lady') and the other photographs are from an album of over 200 by Percy Lankester presented to the Mayor and Mayoress by the guests.

Royal Tunbridge Wells installed its first lady mayor, Councillor Muriel Bury Wells, in May 1949, nominated by Alderman C.E. Westbrook and seconded by Alderman R.H. Burslem. Councillor Miss Wells, seen here in a portrait by Payne Jenkins, served as mayor until 1951 and was elected an alderman in 1952. She served on several council committees, was a governor of local schools, and during the war she served as district head of the Women's Voluntary Service. She was presented at Court shortly before her death in June 1953.

In January 1952 twenty-seven-year-old Royal Tunbridge Wells man Kenneth Dancy was honoured by the Mayor, Alderman F.S. Harries, at a civic reception. Watched by the world's media, Chief Mate Dancy had tried heroically along with Captain Kurt Carlsen to save the sinking American freighter *Flying Enterprise*, although the struggle eventually failed. Speakers at the town hall steps included the Mayor, Admiral Sir Percy Noble, and Gerald Williams, MP, who praised the local celebrity and also the British ocean tug service.

The Mayor, Alderman F.S. Harries, walks in procession to Holy Trinity Church for a service to mark the adoption of three Territorial Army units – 455 (Mixed) Anti-aircraft Regiment, R.A.; H.Q. 133 (Kent and Sussex) Infantry Brigade; and 44 (Home Counties) Divisional Provost Company, Corps of Royal Military Police – by the borough on 16 March 1952 in this *Advertiser* view. Afterwards the Mayor and Brigadier-General T.A.W. Ballard took the salute in Crescent Road.

The Mayor, Councillor John Crabtree, firing the first shot at the new range at Warwick Park on 18 October 1952 in a photograph from the *Advertiser*. The Mayor confessed that he had not held a rifle since the First World War. He scored a bull's-eye, and the target card was later auctioned, realizing £3 5s for Rifle Club funds.

The Mayor and Mayoress, Alderman and Mrs J.A. McNab, entertaining corporation employees and their families at a Mayor's Garden Party at Dunorlan Park on Saturday 18 July 1953. The sun shone and the guests enjoyed themselves rowing on the lake, competing in races, and listening to the Royal Corps of Signals Band. Amongst the prizes awarded by the Mayoress, the Works Department team won the tug-of-war, Mr Roberts won the balloon bursting prize, and Mrs Perry and H. Butcher won at passing-the-hat.

Mr Henry Worthington celebrates his hundredth birthday with the Mayor and Mayoress, Alderman and Mrs McNab, on 24 May 1953 in this *Courier* photograph. Mr Worthington's daughter, Mrs E. Coltman, helps to cut the cake. For thirty-three years Worthington had served as head gardener with the Crown Estate Paving Commissioners. For some time he had special responsibility for the gardens of Carlton Terrace, from which vantage point he had witnessed royal processions from the diamond jubilee of Queen Victoria to the coronation of George V.

Votes are counted in the town hall's council chamber in June 1955 following the general election. Subsequently, the acting deputy returning officer, Alderman F.S. Harries, announced that the Conservative candidate, Gerald Williams, had won by a majority of 10,196 over Labour's Leonard Fagg. Talking to his supporters later, Mr Fagg said that even in Royal Tunbridge Wells, 'the home of wealth and privilege', Labour would win eventually if supporters continued their efforts throughout the division.

Gerald Wellington Williams (1903–89) served as Conservative MP for the Tonbridge division of Kent from 1945 to 1956. After Eton and Cambridge Mr Williams married in 1930 and was serving as a Lieutenant-Commander in the Navy when he first stood for election in July 1945. The highlight of his parliamentary career came in 1952 with the passing of his Private Member's Bill on corneal grafting. Williams applied for the post of Bailiff of the Chiltern Hundreds, i.e. resigned from the House, in 1956 on grounds of ill health.

John Thompson Spare, photographed by Payne Jenkins, moved to Royal Tunbridge Wells in 1946 and was a primary school teacher for forty-two years. Councillor Spare served on the pre-1974 town council and the succeeding borough council from 1953 to 1992, for the last twelve years serving as leader of the council. As mayor of Tunbridge Wells in 1963–4, he was then the youngest person to fill that role. Spare was admitted as an honorary freeman of the borough on 18 April 1986 and was awarded an OBE in the Queen's 1994 birthday honours.

Joint Ladies of the Manor of Rusthall Diana Menuhin and Griselda Kentner were amongst the crowds on the Pantiles for a parade of fashion at the celebrations of the 350th anniversary of the founding of Tunbridge Wells on 8 September 1956. The Ladies were joined in Bath Square by Norman Glanfield to judge the children's fancy dress competition. Their husbands, the musicians Yehudi Menuhin and Louis Kentner, also attended, giving a sell-out concert at the Assembly Hall of well-known piano and violin works.

Alderman Norman Glanfield, accompanied by the town clerk, M.J.H. Girling, signs the declaration of acceptance after being elected as mayor on 23 May 1973 in this *Courier* photograph. Glanfield served as the last mayor of Royal Tunbridge Wells before the authority ceased to exist when the new District of Tunbridge Wells took over in 1974. Alderman Glanfield served on many council committees, was chairman of the town's bench for seven years, and was made an honorary freeman in February 1972.

Alderman Glanfield visits Harris Engineering Company Ltd of Longfield Road on the North Farm Industrial Estate. This firm was one of the first to occupy premises on the estate, the development of which began in the late 1950s. 'This estate,' declared the 1963 town guide, 'pleasantly laid out in rural surroundings and about one and a half miles from the Town Centre, comprises some fifteen or more modern factory buildings well served by approach roads and with all essential services.'

When the 1972 Local Government Act established the new Tunbridge Wells District Council, there was regret that the office of mayor had been replaced by that of chairman. After the charter trustees rejected the option of appointing a purely ceremonial mayor for the town only, the council decided to petition for borough status and the right to elect a mayor for the whole district. Here Councillor G.S. Sturgeon, Mayor, reads the letters patent (dated 20 December 1974) granting borough status.

On 22 March 1977 HM Queen Elizabeth the Queen Mother accepts from the Mayor, Cllr. Myrtle Streeten, the first of a numbered series of medallions commissioned by the borough to commemorate the silver jubilee of HM Queen Elizabeth II and to raise funds for the Silver Jubilee Appeal. Cllr. Mrs Streeten was mayor in 1976–7, a councillor from 1965 to 1991, and was admitted as an honorary freeman of the borough on 2 October 1992.

SECTION TWO
Businesses

The Royal Victoria and Sussex Hotel, where Princess Victoria and her mother the Duchess of Kent spent the last night of their stay in the town in 1834, finally closed in 1880. About ten years later the premises were taken over by William George Harris, furniture remover and warehouseman, whose business had previously been based in Grosvenor Road. The façade of the building remained unaltered, the name at roof level being adapted to read Royal Victoria Pantechnicon. This view dates from 1907.

This photograph by Percy Lankester from 1898/9 shows Frank Davidson's four horse charabanc which ran daily from 19 London Road to take visitors on a tour of the surrounding district. Leaving London Road at 2.30 p.m., the charabanc picked up additional passengers at Daniel Williams' Mount Ephraim Library, seen here at the corner of Mount Ephraim Road. The fare was two shillings and sixpence.

One of the limousines operated in 1939 by the taxi and motor bus hire service of Oliver and Morris Ltd, based at Sladen Chambers in Mount Pleasant, next to Central Station. The business was established in 1919 and survived until 1968, having latterly moved to Goods Station Road. Advertisements offered 'experienced chauffeurs' and declared that 'all our cars have luxuriously comfortable seats, full drop windows and other refinements.'

The Woodlands Laundry at 177 Upper Grosvenor Road, seen here in 1910, was established in 1898 by Misses P.M. and S. Candler. Woodlands was the name of the house in whose grounds the new building was erected. By the time of this picture there was also a branch laundry at Quarry Hill, Tonbridge. The business survived until the early 1960s.

An Edwardian view of the High Rocks Hotel, built in 1839 as a larger replacement for the old inn erected after the 'discovery' of the High Rocks as a tourist attraction by the Duke of York in 1670. The rocks were enclosed as part of the hotel grounds, and the proprietor was traditionally responsible for maintaining and embellishing them. The hotel's original name was the Cape of Good Hope, the change being made by Thomas Coster when he took over in 1899.

One attraction provided by proprietors of the High Rocks Hotel was a trout lake (seen here in 1898/9), excavated about 1850 but now silted up. It was used for boating and skating as well as fishing. According to Thomas Coster's guide, 'whether we cross the bridge and sit upon the island, or lounge in the many nooks upon the margin, or take our turn in the splendid boats, there is a peacefulness and restfulness that will entrance both young and old alike'.

Right: Thomas Coster and his predecessor James Fabian White, proprietor from the 1880s, were particularly active in popularizing the High Rocks. Contemporaries criticized their placard claiming the rocks as 'the grandest sight in England'. They devised several new features, inventing 'ancient legends' to go with them. These included the Devil's Oak and the Wishing Rock, where visitors, as seen here, had to catch three drops of water trickling out of a crack and throw them over their left shoulder while making their wish.

Below: The tradition of providing refreshments among the High Rocks dates back to the earliest days of their popularity, and tea rooms nestling against the cliffs or tucked into clefts appear in various eighteenth-century views. The tea room shown in this 1884 view by George Glanville is probably that described by J. Clifford in 1825 as recently erected. It fell into disuse during the rocks' decline in popularity between the Wars and was converted into an equipment store for climbers.

The Rhododendron Walk in the Old Gardens on the site of the present Old Gardens Close between Birling Road and Forest Road. The gardens (seen here *c.* 1925) were taken over by R. Wallace and Company in 1920, being the remnant of a larger nursery created by Thomas Cripps (whose business was established in 1837) out of the heathland of Frant Forest. Described as 'abounding in specimen trees, rhododendrons, azaleas, Japanese maples and conifers', the Old Gardens were sold for development in 1967.

Wesley Smith standing (left) outside his butcher's shop at 24 Calverley Road (he had another shop at 9 Chapel Place) in 1898/9. He was proud of maintaining the 'good old custom of "Home Killed"' with his slaughterhouse in Varney Street behind Calverley Road. Having arrived in Tunbridge Wells to set up his business in 1895, Wesley Smith was elected to the town council in 1901, and was made an alderman in 1926. He retired from business and public life in 1934, two years before his death.

The south side of Rusthall Road in 1907, with the corner of St Paul's Street in the right foreground. The shops from right to left belonged respectively to Joseph Robertson, butcher; Charles W. Tribe, dairyman; Charles Arthur Fuller, butcher; Frederick Murrell, fishmonger and grocer; and Henry Edward Lash Pilbeam, baker.

The grocery department of the Kent County Stores at 22 (now 48) Mount Pleasant, owned by Walter C. Raiswell Ltd. The shop also sold household equipment and at the time of this picture in 1925 claimed 'lowest competitive prices with up to date efficiency'. The business was established in 1899 in what had been a grocer's store since the 1880s. In the 1930s it expanded to occupy three shop units and finally closed in 1960.

The eighteenth-century wine vaults beneath Turner and Thornton's wine merchant's shop at 58 Mount Ephraim, next to the Mount Ephraim Hotel. This view dates from 1937, two years before the business closed. The vaults consist of a brick-lined passage seventy-five yards long with a well at one end. A.S. Williams, proprietor in the 1930s, linked them with local legends (never substantiated) about a network of tunnels under Mount Ephraim and the Common and speculated about use by smugglers.

The ornate glasshouse in Monson Road, seen here about 1908 with Monson Terrace in the background, was constructed in 1889 for Henry Collyer, florist and nurseryman, whose business was taken over in 1893 by Joseph Haffenden. It has remained in continuous use as a florist's shop to the present day. This view was published as a postcard by James Richards of 85 Camden Road, who was well-known as a publisher of small booklets in Sussex dialect, including sections of the Bible.

The Kent Drug Stores at 48 High Street, seen here in 1898/9, was established in 1892 by F. and G. Chabot. H.S. Pearmund, the second proprietor, described it as 'the first established pharmacy in the town for the supply of medicines, drugs, chemicals, invalid and toilet requisites at store prices for cash'. In 1906 it moved across the road to number 47, where under the name of Lion Drug Store it survived until 1926.

The butcher's shop at 52 Mount Ephraim, near the junction with London Road, was established in the mid-nineteenth century by Thomas White. By the time of this picture in the 1907 town guide, it was occupied by John William Warwick, who took over in the late 1880s. He was succeeded in turn by George Walker (1908), Percy Filmer (1913), Henry Fryer (1924), and Charles Wood (1931). In the 1940s the shop was converted to a private house and the projecting shop front was removed.

Recently named the Old Brew House by its current occupants, the South East England Tourist Board, these premises at 1 Warwick Park were built in 1900 for Pugh and Company, wine merchants previously based at 5 Frant Road. By 1902 the business had been taken over by E. Robins and Company, and in the mid-1930s by Findlater, Mackie, and Company. The building fell vacant in 1967, but by 1969 had been occupied by the toy manufacturers Subbuteo. This view appeared in the 1907 town guide.

Another picture used in the 1907 town guide shows the premises at 10 and 12 Grove Hill Road occupied by Edwin Powell, electrical, motor, and cycle engineer. Powell, who was first established at number 12 in the 1880s, was originally a gunsmith who had diversified into other areas. By 1907 he was claiming '25 years' experience in electric lighting'. He moved to 41 High Street in 1909. Under various names the business survived until 1976/7.

Arguably Tunbridge Wells' most famous shop, Hall's Bookshop (20 & 22 Chapel Place) has been preserved unchanged since moving here in 1938. The original shop, opened by Reuben Hall in 1898, was at number 18. Hall was succeeded in 1922 by Charles Avery, and in 1932 by Harry Pratley, apprenticed to Hall in 1919 and 'among the most highly regarded – and certainly the best loved – booksellers of his generation'. When Pratley retired in 1967, his assistant Elizabeth Bateman took over, to be succeeded in 1983 by her assistant Sabrina Izzard.

In October 1922 the Tradesmen's Association organized Tunbridge Wells Shopping Week to promote the town 'with its handsome establishments and tastefully set out windows' as 'the shopping centre of a very wide district'. One of the week's events was a window-dressing competition, in which the display seen here, at R.W. Weekes at the foot of Mount Pleasant, won second prize in the class for 'Things to Wear (Ladies)'.

One of the earliest modern style plate glass frontages to be seen in the town was erected by Mary Lee's fashion business when it moved into 25–7 (now 56/58/60) Mount Pleasant in 1936. This photograph is contemporary with the opening of what was described at the time as 'a speciality shop of distinction'. The business had been first established in 1932 at 21 High Street. Between 1959 and 1961 the shop expanded, taking in four further units from 48 to 54. It was taken over by Bentalls in 1979.

Thomas Putland first established himself in the town as a corn and coal merchant in 1863, with an office at 54 High Street. In 1892 he diversified into the manufacture of mineral waters, for which he is known today by bottle collectors. A contemporary guide describes his 'extensive and commodious corn stores, coal wharves and aerated water factory' in Goods Station Road. Putland served as a councillor from 1889 and as an alderman from 1900 until his retirement in 1912.

This edible model of the Civic Centre, scaled down to sixteen feet to the inch, was made of fruit cake and icing sugar in 1950 by Harold Robertson at the bakery of John Harrington and Son at 98 Goods Station Road. The total weight of the cake was 30 lb. This well-known local firm which survived until 1985/6 was established in 1904, when John Harrington took over a confectioner's shop called the Bonbonnière at 79 High Street.

The Nevill Bakery in Nevill Street, seen here about 1920, was taken over around 1900 by John Brown, the well-known dairyman, from the previous owner James Botten. A contemporary journalist was greatly impressed by the improvements he made, giving enthusiastic descriptions of ovens which were 'nearly the last word in scientific

excellence' and other examples of new technology. 'In the old days at the Nevill it used to take a man anything over half an hour to knead a sack of flour, but the machine does it better in six minutes.'

Bricks being handmade at the High Brooms Brick and Tile Company's works in 1949. The company, responsible for many of Tunbridge Wells' distinctive brick pavements, had just accepted an order for three million facing bricks for a power station near Brighton: they would take six craftsmen two years to make. The factory (established in 1885) was, together with the gas works, responsible for the early development of High Brooms which began as a cluster of workmen's cottages. The works closed in 1968.

Rock, Hawkins and Thorpe's carriage factory was built in 1892, some six years before this photograph by Percy Lankester. The company, founded as Rock and Son in 1822, had moved from Hastings. Around the turn of the century the firm moved into motor car building and by 1919 was claiming 'one of the best equipped motor works in the kingdom'. Latterly known as Rock, Thorpe and Watson Ltd, it traded until 1946, when it was taken over by Caffyns Ltd.

SECTION THREE
Events

Queen Victoria's diamond jubilee was held on 22 June 1897. After it had been displayed in Alderman Hori Pink's window for several days, the town sent this address to the Queen expressing joy and thankfulness for her long reign. The address was illuminated on vellum by S. Waters of Grosvenor Road and was enclosed within a frame of Tunbridge ware made by Thomas Barton. In July a letter from M.W. Ridley of Whitehall stated that the address had been laid before Her Majesty and that 'I am to inform you that Her Majesty was pleased to receive the same very graciously, and desired me to convey to you an expression of her pleasure at the taste and beauty of the illumination'.

The proclamation of King George V occurred in Royal Tunbridge Wells at 3.00 p.m. on Monday 9 May 1910. A quiet and drenched crowd stood in the rain outside the town hall in Calverley Road to hear the Deputy Mayor, Alderman H.M. Caley, '. . . publish and proclaim, that the high and mighty Prince George Frederick Ernest Albert is now . . . become our only lawful and rightful Liege Lord George the Fifth . . .'. The civic officials then proceeded to read the notice at the Lower Cricket Ground and at the Pantiles, followed in each instance by three cheers for His Majesty and singing of the national anthem.

Royal Tunbridge Wells witnessed massive celebrations for the coronation of George V and Queen Mary on 22 June 1911. Thousands of people filled the streets, which had been decorated with flags, bunting, Venetian masts, and triumphal arches. The events began with a civic service at Holy Trinity Church led by the vicar, Revd D.J. Stather Hunt. This was followed by a meeting on the Common attended by over 5,000 inhabitants. In this photograph, by F.G. Chamney, preparations are made for the twenty-one gun salute at noon, fired by the St James' Church Lads' Brigade.

At 2.00 p.m. on coronation day the Grand Procession commenced. According to the *Tunbridge Wells Advertiser*'s account, 'Never, surely, was there such a pageant, so representative, so brilliant in the splendour of its composition, or so large and effective, in the streets of Tunbridge Wells before!' Over forty floats passed by, including this one, again photographed by Chamney, representing 'The Union of the Rival Roses' by Christ Church School.

Members of Lord De L'Isle and Dudley's troop of Boy Scouts are seen here in a photograph from the *Advertiser* whilst collecting for the Mansion House Fund for the relief of relatives and dependants of casualties of the sinking of the *Titanic* in April 1912. The Scouts drew the attention of residents by playing the large phonograph at street corners throughout the town. Later, the Lord Mayor of London, T.B. Crosby, wrote to the local treasurer for the fund, the Mayor, Colonel Sladen, thanking the town for the magnificent donation of £278 1*s* 6*d*.

The encampment of the Territorial Army on the Lower Cricket Ground on Tunbridge Wells Common in September 1914. The detachment consisted of two signal companies whose duty it was to maintain communication between the various units camped nearby. Rumours developed that the presence of troops implied a danger of imminent invasion by the enemy. However, the military authorities maintained that Royal Tunbridge Wells had been chosen as a headquarters due to its central and commanding position and 'its propinquity to the principal Continental Ports'.

Peace Day celebrations on 19 July 1919 included a massive procession around the town, here seen passing down Mount Pleasant. The procession, marshalled by Chief Constable Prior, included detachments of the borough police, the King's Rifle Corps Cadets, motor cars carrying nurses and wounded soldiers, the Tunbridge Wells Veterans' Association, the Skinners' School Officers' Training Corps, the Boy Scouts, the Post Office, several bands, the Fire Brigade, schoolchildren, and civic dignitaries. The procession followed a circuitous route to the Lower Cricket Ground cheered by thousands of spectators.

Along the route of the Peace Day procession the way was lined with flags, garlands, and triumphal arches. This arch stood at the top of Mount Pleasant hill. The procession was so long that in its detour along Crescent and Monson Roads the tail met the head in front of Calverley Parade. As the mayoral car was brought to a temporary standstill the soldiers and nurses passed by the Mayor and His Worship called for three cheers from the spectators.

Her Highness Princess Helena Victoria (third from the left) is seen here with Lord Richard Nevill, the Camdens, and the Mayor, Councillor Albert Dennis, when they attended the East Sussex and West Kent Musical Festival at the Pump Room, the Pantiles, on 25 March 1931. Her Highness stayed with the Marquis Camden at Bayham Abbey and, after the musical entertainments, took lunch with the Marquess Abergavenny at Eridge Castle. The Acting Mayoress, Miss Dorothy Dennis, presented Her Highness with a Tunbridge ware casket decorated with a view of the castle.

The Prince of Wales began his visit to Royal Tunbridge Wells on 25 July 1928 with luncheon at Bayham Abbey as a guest of the Lord Lieutenant of Kent, Marquis Camden. Here, in a view from the *Advertiser*, the Prince is seated fourth from the right, with the Marchioness Camden to his right and the Marquis behind. Later the Prince and entourage visited the diamond jubilee show of the Tunbridge Wells and Southern Counties' Agricultural Society and evidently enjoyed leaving the royal box to meet several 'old and trusty tillers of the soil'.

After the show the Prince was greeted by the Mayor, Councillor Septimus Parsonage, as he arrived to open officially the Cadogan Playing Field. Girl Guides and Boy Scouts formed a guard of honour as the Prince opened the gates with a gold key, witnessed by 2,400 children and numerous official guests. Here the Prince is seen chatting to E.J. Strange, who had donated the field to the town, and the Mayor following the opening.

Queen Mary came to town on 11 July 1932 during a private visit to see Dowager Lady Hillingdon, a former lady-in-waiting. However, news of her arrival travelled quickly, and over a thousand people converged upon the Pantiles and surrounding roads to witness the Queen shopping. The royal party spent most of their time in antique shops, the Queen adding a casket, a cribbage board, a view of the Pantiles, and an inkwell with a view of Eridge Castle to her own Tunbridge ware collection.

During the Duchess of York's visit to the town on 19 July 1932 she inspected a guard of honour of the 4th (Queen's Own) Royal West Kent Regiment accompanied by Colonel G.S. Crossman, Lieutenant-Colonel F.H. Hancock, Captain Sir Derrick Watson, and the Marquis Camden before laying the foundation stone of the Kent and Sussex Hospital.

In this photograph from the *Advertiser* the Mayor, Councillor E.B. Weekes, is seen planting one of two red chestnut trees near Fonthill to commemorate the silver jubilee of the accession of George V and Queen Mary on 6 May 1935. In order that town traders could share in the honour, the second chestnut was planted by N.C. Yates, president of the Chamber of Trade. The national anthem was sung. Later, a service of thanksgiving was held at Calverley Grounds.

The proclamation of the accession of King Edward VIII is read outside the town hall by the Mayor of Royal Tunbridge Wells, Councillor E.B. Weekes, accompanied by members, magistrates, and civic officials, on 22 January 1936. Across the street, reports the *Courier*, 'all classes rubbed shoulder to shoulder in the spirit of loyalty and sympathy, yet at the same time inwardly thankful for the accession of a democratic Prince as King of England'. The ceremony was repeated at the Pantiles.

In this *Courier* photograph the Duke of Kent is introduced to officers of the Tunbridge Wells Council of Voluntary Service before cutting a silk ribbon to officially open a development of homes intended for the elderly during his visit to the town on 23 June 1938. E.L. Edmunds, joint honorary secretary of the council, was honoured for his many years of social work by having the estate named Sherborne Close, Sherborne being his birthplace. The Duke toured the homes before the Bishop of Rochester led a service of dedication.

The Civic Centre's Assembly Hall theatre was opened by the Marchioness Camden on 24 May 1939 as part of the celebrations of the jubilee of incorporation of Tunbridge Wells. Here, in an *Advertiser* view, the Marchioness receives the architect, Percy Thomas. Several of the principal contractors for the Civic Centre works were local firms – Corben & Son (the building), Baltic Saw Mills (timber), F. Malpass & Son (iron), High Brooms Brick and Tile Co. (facing bricks), Hall & Co. (ballast and sand), and F. Blundell (haulage).

Later on Wednesday 24 May, in this *Advertiser* view, the Charter Queen, Miss Meryl Maldwyn Jones, passes through the crowd on the Pantiles after being crowned by Miss June Duprez, star of the recently released film *Four Feathers*. Later the Charter Queen joined a carnival procession to a fun fair at Down Farm, opened by the Mayor and Mayoress, Alderman and Mrs C.E. Westbrook. Other celebrations during Charter Week included a 'Pageant of the Pantiles', a Charter Dance, and a grand firework display at the fairground.

This photograph, taken in Calverley Grounds, from the 30 August 1940 issue of the *Courier* was captioned, 'Crater caused by a high explosive bomb which was dropped in the pleasure grounds of a South East Town'. A lone raider had resulted in nine bombs falling on Royal Tunbridge Wells. Having just concluded a patrol of the grounds, Messrs Bean and Cogger, two special constables, stepped into the thatched tea-house for a break. As the scream of bombs was heard, they threw themselves to the ground, emerging later covered in plaster and debris and 'looking like two floury millers'.

Following sightings of a lone reconnaissance aircraft cruising at 5,000 to 6,000 feet altitude, on 12 September 1940 at 5.10 p.m. came a heavy bombing raid causing considerable damage to the Kent and Sussex Hospital, a garage used by American ambulances, and the presbytery of St Augustine's Church. Incendiary bombs fell in Lansdowne Road, Calverley Street, and on the Culverden Golf Club. The raid resulted in twenty-seven casualties – twelve killed and fifteen seriously injured. Ninety-six properties were damaged.

Marquis Camden is seen taking the salute at the march past outside the new town hall before the opening of Tunbridge Wells War Weapons Week by Marchioness Camden and the wartime Mayor, Alderman Westbrook, on 7 December 1940 in this *Advertiser* view. Residents were asked to invest in war bonds, defence bonds, or savings certificates totalling £500,000 in order that additional bombers could be bought. Two weeks later the Mayor thanked the town, announcing that £510,224 15s 9d had been collected for the war effort.

A battered Messerschmitt 109 fighter is delivered to the new museum building for exhibition during the 1940 War Weapons Week. The display also included a selection of bombs (the largest one, named Satan, weighing over two tons), parts of German aircraft, a collapsible dinghy, a parachute, and posters and models by local schoolchildren. Although the exhibition was housed inside the library and museum building, the war itself meant that neither the library nor museum took up residence until after the conflict.

The only occasion on which George VI visited Royal Tunbridge Wells officially was on 14 June 1941 when he met and lunched with Field Marshal Lord Montgomery, then a general, at the 12 Corps headquarters at Broadwater Down. Seen behind the King in this *Advertiser* view are General Sir Bernard Paget and Montgomery.

Soldiers of 12 Corps stand on the crane of a Crossley three ton lorry to suspend camouflage netting over the road adjacent to Montgomery's headquarters at 10 Broadwater Down. There has been much speculation over the possible connection between the headquarters and the network of tunnels excavated under Hargate Forest nearby in 1940–1, under conditions of great secrecy. Montgomery denied one theory that they had been constructed for him as an underground control centre. Another suggestion has been that they were made to harbour resistance fighters in the event of an invasion.

In this *Courier* view three-year-old Ronnie demonstrates to Princess Margaret how to ride a rocking horse during her inspection, as President of Dr Barnardo's, of St Christopher's Nursery Training College on Pembury Road on Tuesday 19 October 1948. The Princess stayed for an hour and a half touring the grounds and observing 'the inmates – staff and children' – at work and play. She had received a warm welcome to the town, with school children waving Union Jacks and cheering crowds lining every pavement as the royal Daimler passed by.

The famous 'Pantiles gap' of missing buildings from numbers thirty to thirty-six was created in 1937 when the houses were demolished due to their dilapidated condition. The town council intended either to lay out a garden or to construct a brick wall to conceal the gap for the foreseeable future. When the garden scheme fell after a one vote defeat, the Pantiles Association stepped in to create the garden itself. Here, on 8 August 1951, the garden is opened by the Mayor, Alderman Frank Harries.

A large crowd gathered outside the town hall at noon on 8 February 1952 to hear the Mayor, Alderman Harries, read the proclamation of accession of Elizabeth II. In wording similar to the previous proclamations of this century, Harries announced that, 'the High and Mighty Princess Elizabeth Alexandra Mary is now, by the death of our late Sovereign of Happy Memory, become Queen Elizabeth the Second, by the Grace of God Queen of this Realm and of all Her other realms and territories . . .'.

This view from the *Advertiser* shows part of the 'Bohemian atmosphere on the Pantiles' during the new open air summer art exhibition there organized by the Entertainments and Publicity Committee in 1952. The entertainments manager, R.J. Powell, hoped that the exhibition could become an annual event. Today the annual show continues in popularity both with the public and with the amateur and professional artists who take the opportunity to display their works.

The newly inaugurated Mayor, Alderman J.A. McNab, returns to the town hall following the civic service at Holy Trinity Church on 24 May 1953 in this *Courier* photograph. Preceded by the mace bearer, the procession included bands of the Sea Cadet Corps and Air Training Corps, and representatives of the British Legion, the Royal Signals Association, the St John Ambulance Brigade, and the Special Constabulary. The service had been conducted by Revd A.J. Brown, Canon H.W. Thomas, and Revd T. Helm.

The streets throughout Royal Tunbridge Wells were decorated gaily for the coronation festivities of Elizabeth II on 2 June 1953. Here, in a photograph by R.J. Glass, the length of Calverley Road is decorated with garlands suspended from floral crowns. On Coronation Day itself most Tunbridge Wells events were confined to the evening when a great crowd assembled for the fancy-dress parade, to hear the Queen's message broadcast, to watch the bonfire and fireworks, and to take part in community singing.

In another view by Glass the decorated High Street is seen. In the early hours of Coronation Day the police apprehended two Tunbridge Wells men for stealing coronation flags. Subsequently they were each fined £7 with 5s costs for stealing five flags worth £2 9s. One of the men was already on two years' probation for receiving lead stolen from Pembury Church. For breach of probation the man was sentenced to one day's imprisonment.

During the week of the coronation a variety of events and festivities were held throughout the town and district. In this *Advertiser* photograph, on 4 June the Deputy Mayor, Councillor John Crabtree, attends the children's street party at Tunnel and Belgrave Roads. Several other street parties were held, mostly organized by committees of street residents. At Summervale Road 220 children attended. The day included a fancy-dress parade, tea, a procession around Ramslye Estate, community singing, and a display of trick cycling.

The Tunbridge Wells Sea Cadet Corps held a fête at Down Farm on 3 August 1953, and here the Mayoress, Mrs J.A. McNab, is seen with fancy-dress entrant Brenda Pratt of Upper Grosvenor Road. Disappointingly, in this first event on the programme, only two children entered the competition, Miss Pratt as a salad, and Patricia Eade as a Christmas cracker. Both girls were awarded prizes.

The Mayor, Alderman J.A. McNab, lays a wreath at the Royal Tunbridge Wells War Memorial following the Service of Remembrance on 8 November 1953 in this *Courier* view. War widows and representatives from military and ex-Service organizations were assembled in the light rain along with Gerald Williams, MP, and civic councillors and officers. The service was conducted by Revd A.W. Habershon of Holy Trinity Church and Revd Thomas Helm of St Andrew's. Before the two minutes' silence, the assembly sang the hymns 'O God, our help in ages past' and 'O God of Jacob, by Whose hand Thy people still are fed'.

Twenty-five American Civil Air Patrol cadets were entertained to a civic luncheon on 11 August 1953 as part of an annual exchange scheme. Later they were conducted around Penshurst Place by Councillor Rupert Gunnis. Just before leaving the US, many for the first time, President Eisenhower had told them to go into British homes where they would meet people just as great as themselves. During their brief visit they did live with local residents.

At Christmas, 1953, the Mayor, Alderman McNab, and Tunbridge Wells Rotarians are seen outside the town hall just before setting off to deliver 130 free Christmas dinners to bedridden and housebound elderly people in this *Advertiser* photograph. Each parcel, costing 5s 2d, contained a pre-cooked and frozen meal of soup, chicken, Brussels sprouts, potatoes, and Christmas pudding. The meals could be warmed for eating in just twenty minutes.

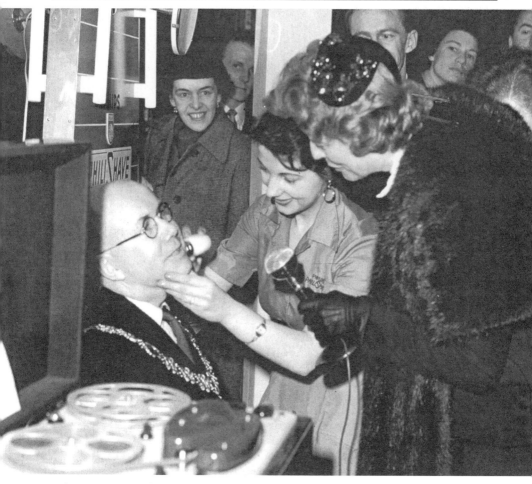

Television personality Miss Joan Gilbert opened the Tunbridge Wells Trades Fair on
20 February 1954, and crowds of residents attended to catch a glimpse of the star. After
the opening the president of the Chamber of Trade, Graham Weekes, the Mayor,
Alderman J.A. McNab, and Miss Gilbert toured the stands. As seen in this *Courier*
photograph, at the stand of Messrs Featherstone, 'Miss Gilbert interviewed the Mayor
on a tape recorder while attractive Miss Patrice Fitzgerald was shaving him with an
electric razor'.

The Mayor intended to make a speech to officially open the Women's Royal Army Corps recruiting campaign on 30 January 1954, but a snow blizzard intervened. Instead, he inspected radar equipment parked outside the library and museum building. Several commanding officers escort the Mayor as he inspects radar, predictor, and plotting equipment manned by WRAC members in this *Courier* photograph.

The Tunbridge Wells and South Eastern Counties' Agricultural Society was founded in 1862 though first known as the Tunbridge Wells, Groombridge and Borders of Kent and Sussex Agricultural Association. The new association resolved to relocate the existing agricultural show from Groombridge to Tunbridge Wells, and the first Tunbridge Wells show was held in October at Folly Field, near the Pump Room. In 1881 the show moved to more spacious grounds near the West Station. From 1890 the show was usually held in July.

Penny is seen with her mistress, fifteen-year-old Dorothy Francis, at the centenary agricultural show held on 17–18 July 1962 in this *Courier* photograph. The centenary show was visited by the Queen Mother, who had last attended as Duchess of York in 1932. She was accompanied by the Abergavennys, the Marquess being president of the show society. The Queen Mother presented many prizes, and later a near stampede was caused as spectators followed her open field car as she drove to view the trade stands and floral displays.

Five-year-old Brenda Hardes, of Staplehurst, helps her father by brushing down his pigs at the centenary show. Although a centenary, there had not been one hundred shows. There were no shows from 1915 to 1919 when the showground was requisitioned by the military. Foot and mouth disease struck twice, in 1927 and 1952, though in the latter case only the classes for cloven hooves were cancelled. Then, again, in 1939 the War Department required the land, causing the show to move from Eridge Road for 1947 to 1950.

Traffic ground to a halt outside the town hall in September 1969 in this *Advertiser* picture as a convoy of four baby elephants made their way along Crescent and Church Roads. The elephants had an appointment on the Common with Sir Robert Fossett's circus, which stayed in town for three days. A traffic warden accompanied them to avoid problems with the usual motorized traffic.

A Declaration of Friendship was signed linking Tunbridge Wells with Wiesbaden, West Germany, when Herr Rudi Schmitt, Oberbürgermeister of Wiesbaden, visited on 15 April 1971. In this photograph Herr Schmitt (right) and Mayor of Tunbridge Wells Alderman Ronald Woodland shake hands after the signing as the town clerk, M.J.H. Girling, holds up the treaty. The friendship had begun ten years earlier when Tunbridge Wells war veterans began an acquaintance with veterans at Wiesbaden. The relationship was strengthened by a Twinning Alliance declaration on 22 April 1989.

A scene from the 1967 Paramount film *Half a Sixpence* being shot on the Pantiles with appropriate period props and extras. Directed by George Sidney, the film starred Tommy Steele, who played Kipps, a draper's assistant who inherits a fortune, and was based upon a novel of that name by H.G. Wells.

International subscriber dialling was introduced to the Tunbridge Wells telephone area at an inaugural ceremony at Telephone House, Church Road, on 6 August 1976. Here the Mayor, Cllr. Myrtle Streeten, accompanied by her husband, Francis Streeten, makes the first direct-dialled call to members of her family in Perth, Western Australia.

Following the 1974 reorganization of local government, application was made to the Earl Marshall for a grant of arms to the new Borough of Tunbridge Wells. Upon completion of the work by the College of Arms, Somerset Herald, Rodney Dennys, presented it to the Mayor, Cllr. Myrtle Streeten, at a council meeting on 5 October 1976. Somerset Herald had designed the new arms with the assistance of Cllr. Mrs Streeten and Francis Streeten.

SECTION FOUR

Public Services

The Mayor, Alderman James McNab, visits the Vale Road post office to see the sorting of the Christmas mail on 21 December 1953. The town's general post office moved to these premises in 1895, having previously been located on the Pantiles. At the time of its construction the new building was criticized for not having its main façade facing the Common, from which it was most visible. The building also housed a telephone exchange from 1915 to 1965. This picture was published in the *Courier*.

The first council houses at Sherwood Park nearing completion in October 1952. A shortage of housing after the Second World War had led the council to embark on a building programme which was 'among the most ambitious and carefully laid in the country'. The Sherwood project was the third stage in this development. The first estate of 120 houses was begun at Power Mill Lane in 1946. The second, at Ramslye, was begun in 1948, and within six years this estate consisted of 418 dwellings.

Councillor Stanley Muffett (mayor 1955–7) opens on 6 January 1956 the thousandth council house built by Tunbridge Wells Corporation since the war. With him are the new tenants, Mr and Mrs P. Fearis and their two daughters Alma (left) and Susan, who had moved into the two bedroomed house at 62 Bracken Road on the Sherwood estate the previous day. 'They are delighted with their new home,' reported the *Advertiser*, 'and Alma in particular loves the bathroom – something they did not have in their previous home.'

The Borough Technical Institute in Monson Road, now the Adult Education Centre, was opened by Lord Avebury in 1902. As an institution it originated from classes held by Dr George Abbott at the Ear and Eye Hospital, moving about 1889 to its own premises at Walmer House on Mount Sion. In 1894 it moved to 42 Calverley Road, where instruction was given in 'art, land & engineering surveying, levelling &c., architectural design & sanitary building, wood carving, cookery, dress making, iron work, drawing, French &c.'

On the staircase of the new Technical Institute are three stained glass windows by Dudley Forsyth of London with allegorical figures representing Science, Industry, Art, and Commerce. These were presented by Alderman C.R. Fletcher Lutwidge, himself an artist, who was a great supporter and instrumental in acquiring purpose built premises. There was much disappointment when, only a year after opening, new national legislation transferred the institute from local management to the care of Kent County Council.

Murray House, Berkeley Road, Mount Sion, on the left of this 1934 photograph by D.J. Johnson, was purchased in 1858 by William Law Pope, Minister of King Charles' Church, for the girls of his church school. An extension was opened in 1909. The school continued until in 1953 it was incorporated in the new Bennett Memorial School, whose first year pupils used the building for a few years more. On the right is Berkeley Place, built as a lodging house in 1699.

The Archbishop of Canterbury, Dr Geoffrey Fisher, is received by the Mayor (Alderman McNab) on the occasion of the opening and dedication of Bennett Memorial School for Girls at Culverden Down on 18 November 1953. The building of the school had been made possible by a gift and loan from Lady Bennett, who laid the foundation stone on 17 October 1951. To give an opportunity for local residents to hear him, the archbishop addressed a mass meeting at the Assembly Hall in the evening.

Tunbridge Wells Borough Police, photographed *c*. 1923 by Ambrose Stickells of Camden Road. Many of the men seen here in the yard of the old Police Station (occupied in 1846) in Calverley Road are proudly wearing their First World War medals. In the centre of the front seated row is Chief Constable S.A. Hector, appointed in 1921; on his right is Guy Carlton who succeeded him in 1927. The town force, formed in 1835, remained independent until amalgamated with the Kent County Constabulary in 1943.

The setting up of the 22nd Battalion (Tunbridge Wells) Home Guard (initially Local Defence Volunteer Force) began in May 1940. Its first commanding officer was Brigadier General Henry Knox, who organized separate companies for each ward. He was succeeded in July 1941 by Brigadier General Reginald Manley Sims, who was already working as an assistant to General Sir Cecil Romer, whose regional headquarters based successively in Frant Road and Broadwater Down was responsible for Home Guard organization throughout Kent, Sussex and Surrey.

The Central Station in 1880, showing on the right the building facing Mount Pleasant which was replaced by the present structure in 1912. On the Vale Road side the original building of 1846 has been preserved. The first train to Tunbridge Wells, bearing local dignitaries and leading figures in the railway company, together with a brass band, arrived on 19 September 1845 at the temporary Jack Wood station near the present Grosvenor Bridge. The line was then extended through a tunnel into the town centre.

High Rocks Halt, on the line out of the West Station to Brighton, was opened on 1 June 1907 to provide an alternative means of transport to this well-known beauty spot, popular as a day's outing for tourists staying at Tunbridge Wells. The down platform is in the background on the east side of the bridge, which carries High Rocks Lane over the line. The halt continued in use until 5 May 1952.

Three open-topped motor buses belonging to Autocar Services Ltd wait outside the company's office in the Opera House building about 1925. In the mid-1920s there was intense rivalry between Autocar and Redcar Services Ltd of Monson Road. Buses of the two companies often raced each other to pick up passengers, and there were allegations of obstruction and attempts to force rival vehicles off the road. Both companies were bought up by Maidstone and District Motor Services in 1935.

An Autocar Services bus on Mount Pleasant in 1923. In 1924 the Chief Constable reported that the borough's 102 buses were causing serious congestion in the town centre. The rival companies were operating buses 'unaccounted for in the timetables and additional to the needs of the public' in order to engage in 'competitive touting for customers'. Buses would appear at stops '20 or 30 minutes before their scheduled time of departure, stop five minutes, drive away and return again a very short time afterwards.'

Lankester's view of the London and Counties Distributing Company's second goods car delivering in Tunbridge Wells on 8 June 1901. The first car had been greeted with a great celebration the previous day, but the vehicle seen here broke down on the way and arrived a day late. Edward T. Hughes, grocer and wine merchant, organized the experimental service from London 'having for years suffered inconvenience and exasperating delays at the hands of the railway companies'. Long distance freight transport by motor vehicles was an innovation, and the scheme attracted interest throughout the country.

Grosvenor Bridge pictured by Ron Glass prior to rebuilding in 1968. The original structure was opened on 7 March 1883 by Mrs John Stone Wigg, wife of the chairman of the local board. The arches seen in the foreground served for many years from 1887 as the town mortuary. A journalist wrote in 1904: 'Those dark, ill ventilated arches under the Grosvenor Bridge have, it is true, an inquisitorial atmosphere, but they form a repulsive place in which to hold inquests.'

Part of the High Brooms Gas Works photographed by Mary Page in May 1969 following their closure two years earlier. The buildings were decorated with 5 ft. square terracotta plaques, two of which can be seen here, representing gasholders with cross torches above. The works moved here in 1880 from its original site (dating from the formation of the local gas company in 1834) in Golding Street behind Calverley Road, on part of the land now occupied by Royal Victoria Place.

Cooling towers on the site of the original generating station of the Municipal Electricity Undertaking between Quarry Road and the railway. Established by the town council, the system was inaugurated by the Mayor, Sir David Salomons, on 9 October 1895. After a reception at the Camden Hall, the Mayoress switched on the power and the local yeomanry escorted a procession to the town hall. The station remained in council ownership until 1947 and closed in 1969, about the time of this view by Ron Glass.

The Municipal Electricity Undertaking's entry in the parade and competition for commercial vehicles held on 3 October 1928 during Britain and Empire Week. The week's events were organized under the auspices of the Chamber of Trade to encourage support for the industries of Britain and the Empire. It was inaugurated on 1 October by Sir James Parr, High Commissioner for New Zealand, at a ceremony in Calverley Grounds attended by over two thousand people.

In this view from the *Electrical Engineer* workmen are seen laying a cable outside the Great Hall, Mount Pleasant, for the municipal telephone system which the town council, urged on by the Tradesmen's Association (dissatisfied with the performance of the National Telephone Company) and inspired by the success of a similar undertaking in Guernsey, had agreed to establish. The system was inaugurated by Alderman Frank Green, Lord Mayor of London, on 27 July 1901. It was strongly opposed by a Ratepayers' League founded in 1902 by Colonel T.J. Holland to campaign against 'municipal trading'.

The switch room in the municipal telephone exchange in Calverley Parade. In 1902 the council requested permission from the Local Government Board to raise a further loan towards the telephone system. Opponents forcefully expressed their views at a public enquiry and at an investigation by the Local Government Board's Auditor. The council was vindicated, but nonetheless decided to allow a takeover by the National Telephone Company. The Ratepayers' League then launched an unsuccessful campaign to sell off the municipal electricity system.

Inside the new Automatic Telephone Exchange, Trunk Switching Centre, and Repeater Station in St John's Road, prior to its official opening by A. Wolstencroft, Deputy General Director of the GPO, on 22 February 1965. This facility replaced three manual exchanges, one opened in 1915 at the post office building in Vale Road, a relief exchange opened on the St John's Road site in 1947, and a third at Southborough.

The official opening of the Tunbridge Wells Corporation's new waterworks at Saints Hill near Fordcombe by the Mayor, Councillor Albert Dennis, on 5 October 1931. Here an electrically driven pump drew water from a 407 foot borehole tapping the water-bearing Ashdown Sands. Ever since the establishment of a municipal water supply system in 1865, the town had suffered from periodic shortages in dry summers and each apparent solution to the problem proved in its turn to be only temporary.

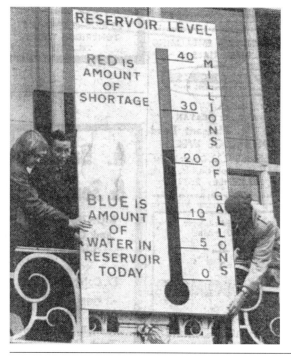

Workmen erect an indicator of the water level in the Pembury Reservoir on the town hall balcony on 30 April 1973. The local press (this picture is from the *Advertiser*) announced 'the gravest water crisis in the town's history', with threats of rationing and standpipes in the streets. Rain and a drop in consumption averted such measures, but the council decided that an independent water undertaking could no longer be maintained. In October it was taken over by the Sevenoaks and Tonbridge Water Company.

The Ear and Eye Hospital on Mount Sion, photographed by D.J. Johnson in 1934, the year in which it was incorporated in the new Kent and Sussex Hospital. Supported by voluntary contributions, it was founded in 1878 by Dr George Abbott as the Ear and Eye Dispensary with premises in Vale Road. In 1888 it moved to part of the old Royal Sussex Hotel in the Pantiles, and finally in 1900 to Mount Sion.

Sherwood Park Clinic and Spa opened in 1931 in the former home of Sir William Siemens, pioneer of electrical engineering. Following the discovery of a spring in the grounds with 'curative properties unsurpassed in any other water', ambitious plans were put forward for grandiose new buildings. There was great excitement and talk of a revival of Royal Tunbridge Wells as 'Europe's foremost spa'. The local press predicted 'a new era of prosperity, employment for 1,000 people and possibilities of 200,000 visitors a year'.

The Kent and Sussex Hospital is opened by Marchioness Camden on 25 July 1934. It was designed to supersede the old General Hospital in Grosvenor Road and the Ear and Eye Hospital on Mount Sion. Costing £150,000, it was then the largest building project ever carried out in Royal Tunbridge Wells and neighbourhood. The site had been purchased in 1926 and work commenced on 6 June 1932. Initially the hospital operated as a charity, supported largely by subscriptions, donations, and public fund-raising efforts.

The Mayoress, Mrs McNab, is introduced as the vice president of the local division of the St John Ambulance Nursing Cadets on 25 September 1953. She is seen presenting a writing set to Sgt. Audrey Emerton who was leaving the division to take up nurse training. The St John Ambulance brigade occupied the former headquarters of the Volunteer Fire Brigade next to the swimming baths in Monson Road.

The Homoeopathic Hospital was established in 1863 as the Homoeopathic Dispensary. Initially in the High Street opposite Christ Church, it later moved to Vale Road, and around 1890 to the southern end of Upper Grosvenor Road. In 1903 it transferred to the new premises seen here, which were designed by local architect C.H. Strange. This view from London Road was taken by D.J. Johnson in 1934.

Before the development of an effective public library service, private lending libraries flourished. Seen here in 1907 is the Royal Library (named because of patronage by the Duchess of Kent) in the High Street, established in 1841 by John Colbran (the local guide publisher). His son St John Colbran sold it in 1887 to Henry Goulden, who successively took into partnership Edward Nye and (from 1894) Stanley Curry. The library closed in 1949, but Goulden and Curry's bookselling and stationery business continued until 7 June 1986.

The floral clock which was maintained for many years at the corner of Mount Pleasant Road and Monson Road, seen here in a photograph of about 1955 by Sydney Lazell. Behind is the entrance to the library and museum building which was officially opened by Lord De L'Isle and Dudley on 27 October 1952. The former library in Dudley Road, adopted by the council in 1921 from the Mechanics' Institute, had closed on 4 October. Although the shell of the building had been completed by the outbreak of the Second World War, fitting out had been long delayed. The museum did not move in until 1954.

Gardeners preparing a new display depicting the emblem of the Festival of Britain at the Mount Pleasant entrance to Calverley Grounds in June 1951. The grounds were purchased by the council from the Calverley Estate in 1920 and landscaped and fitted out over the course of the next six years. The originally thatched tea house in the background was built in 1924 along with the bandstand, bowling green pavilion, and entrance lodge. The recently burned down tennis pavilion dated from 1922.

The bandstand in Grosvenor Recreation Ground was given by Councillor Edward Elvy Robb in memory of his father and survived until 1935. It was opened on 7 September 1899 by the Mayor, Alderman Frank William Stone, before a performance by the Borough Band under conductor M. Marks. Marks had been hired by the Band Committee in 1896 so that the existing band could be 'licked into shape'. Some members were replaced, causing much resentment and angry correspondence in the local press.

Grosvenor Recreation Ground was opened in 1889, although landscaping was not complete until the following year. According to a contemporary guide, 'The juvenile portion of the population think there is no such charm as is found here feeding the swans, and then gamboling on the sloping banks of this delightful place, which . . . is well wooded and altogether a place of beauty.' This view from about 1905 shows the two ornamental ponds in the hollow at the northern end which were filled in in 1934.

The southern end of Grosvenor Recreation Ground is on the site of the former Calverley Waterworks, which was combined with land donated by John Stone Wigg, the town's first mayor, in 1887. The pond seen here about 1906 is the only one which survives today. At the far end, to the left of the island, are a series of ornamental 'grottoes' or 'dripping wells' created to give the impression of shallow caves with water trickling down the rocks.

Hilbert Recreation Ground, seen here in the 1937 town guide, adjoins Grosvenor Recreation Ground and was given to the town in 1931 (with an addition in 1937) by Edward Jeffery Strange (mayor 1936–7) in memory of his mother Lydia Hilbert. It was part of Charity Farm (formerly Packs-in-the-Wood). Apart from the football pitches and some mown grassland, the land has been preserved in its original state. It contains two small woods, Folly Shaw and Roundabout Wood, with streams running through them.

Dunorlan Park, originally the landscaped grounds of Henry Reed's 1862 mansion, was purchased by the town council in 1945 and opened in 1946. An 1872 sale brochure describes the view seen here (*c.* 1905) as 'a luxuriant avenue of Deodaras and Douglas Picea, leading from an elegant Grecian temple to a handsome stone basin and fountain'. The mansion, requisitioned for the war effort, did not pass to the council until the War Damage Commission vacated it in 1957. It was then sold for development and subsequently demolished.

The Grove bandstand, seen here about 1910, was acquired from Warrior Square, St Leonards, and inaugurated by the Mayor, Alderman C.R. Fletcher Lutwidge, on 24 May 1897. On 22 September the Borough Band performed at an 'illuminated fête' when 'over 7,000 coloured lamps and Chinese lanterns were brought into service' and the 'night's display was almost Parisian in variety, beauty and extent'. Neglected after the Grove was requisitioned by the military during the Second World War, the bandstand was demolished in 1946.

SECTION FIVE

Commons

Sheep graze on Tunbridge Wells Common near St Helena (built 1828–38), one of three picturesque cottages built on to rock outcrops between London Road and Mount Ephraim on the site of older structures pre-dating the Rusthall Manor Act of 1739 (which protected the Commons against further encroachment without mutual consent of the Lord of the Manor and the Freeholders). This postcard view was published by the local Photochrom Company around 1906.

The westernmost and oldest of the three rock built cottages is Gibraltar, seen here from Mount Ephraim. It was built between 1814 and 1824 on the site of an earlier cottage of the same name. Like many of the town's older houses, it was originally used as a lodging house. By the time of this photograph, taken around 1960 by Harold Betteridge, it had fallen into a state of dilapidation. It was threatened with demolition, but was eventually restored in 1970–1.

Local photographer George Glanville, whose work is prominent in late Victorian town guides, would have been standing by Gibraltar Cottage when taking this distant view of the hillock of Mount Edgcumbe, named after Emma, Dowager Countess of Mount Edgcumbe, who spent the summers of 1795–7 in the town. The picture dates from the 1890s and shows in the middle distance to the left the Lower Cricket Ground, levelled and railed in 1885–6. It had earlier been the informal playing field of Romanoff House School in London Road and the site of an annual bonfire on 5 November.

Ephraim Lodge, the southernmost of the three buildings on Mount Edgcumbe, and in origin an early eighteenth-century lodging house, stands at the far left of this popular Victorian and Edwardian prospect looking across the Lower Cricket Ground towards Gibraltar Cottage. To the right, at the nearest corner of the Cricket Ground, can be seen the protective enclosure around the recently planted oak tree commemorating Queen Victoria's golden jubilee in 1887.

The three buildings on Mount Edgcumbe appear on the earliest map of the town by John Bowra in 1738. In this postcard by local publisher Harold Camburn they are seen from near Wellington Rocks to the west. On the right is Ephraim Lodge with its terrace commanding an elevated view of the Common, in the centre Mount Edgcumbe Cottage, and on the left another eighteenth-century lodging house, now Mount Edgcumbe Hotel. The Arctic explorer Sir William Parry stayed there in 1839.

This popular postcard illustration by Valentine and Sons of Dundee dates originally from the late 1890s. It looks across Castle Road and the Lower Cricket Ground, with Mount Ephraim behind. At this period the Common was maintained as open heathland by the grazing of sheep and cattle belonging to the freehold tenants of the Manor of Rusthall. Grazing continued until at least the late 1920s. The Freeholders were responsible for managing the Commons until the establishment of the Conservators in 1890.

'The Common is a glorious substitute for the sea front of other towns', declared the 1903 town guide. Following a campaign by the Tradesmen's Association and others, the Freeholders' Committee agreed in 1881 to level a strip of land along the northern edge of the Common to create a turf walk. The Mount Ephraim Promenade, seen here about 1908, proved so popular with residents and visitors that it had to be gravelled in 1891 and finally asphalted in 1925.

Charles II and Queen Katharine stayed at Mount Ephraim House in 1663 while their court camped on the Common. Little of the original structure survives, since the house was substantially rebuilt in the nineteenth century, acquiring a new façade in the 1840s. Together with the Chalet (on the right in this *c.* 1970 view), built in its grounds around 1800, it was the Tunbridge ware manufactory of William Fenner from the 1790s to 1840. He was succeeded in turn by Edmund Nye and Thomas Barton.

Wellington Rocks, illustrated here in a souvenir album of about 1895, were named after the Wellington Hotel, which stands behind on Mount Ephraim. The hotel was opened in 1875 by John Braby, a great admirer of the Duke of Wellington. Earlier names for the rocks include Castle Rock, probably deriving from the long vanished Castle Tavern of 1665–70, although there is a possibility that the tavern was named after the rock, whose highest point might have been thought to resemble a castle tower.

Sheep graze undisturbed by players on the Higher Cricket Ground. Although cricket was played on this site informally from the mid-eighteenth century, it was not officially set apart for the purpose until 1839, when the newly formed Tunbridge Wells Cricket Club received permission from the Freeholders to use and improve it, and to erect notices to deter abuse of the turf. The ground was subsequently enlarged in 1859 and 1875. This view is from a lantern slide of about 1890.

After persistent lobbying by local groups such as the Tradesmen's Association, the Conservators agreed in 1907 to erect the first thatched timber shelter on Tunbridge Wells Common between Fir Tree Pond and the Spa Hotel. In 1908 they authorized two more, one near the Higher Cricket Ground and one south of Victoria Grove. The first was destroyed by a flying bomb in 1944, with the death of an elderly resident. The other two succumbed to decay and vandalism in the 1950s.

Royal Victoria Grove was planted in 1835 to commemorate the visits of Princess Victoria with her mother the Duchess of Kent. The old Queen's Grove nearby, planted in 1702 for the coronation of Queen Anne and replanted in 1811, had never done well and was by that time dying. Victoria Grove was planned as a double avenue of sycamores, limes, and elms. The elms succumbed to disease in 1972, and in 1992 the third row was replanted to celebrate the fortieth anniversary of Elizabeth II's accession.

Local photographer, artist, and naturalist Harold Betteridge spent many hours exploring Tunbridge Wells and Rusthall Commons, and between 1962 and 1964 he compiled a three volume photographic record of them. This view shows part of the racecourse on Tunbridge Wells Common, a feature which appears on the earliest town map of 1738. Race meetings were held for two days each year, in August and September, but were discontinued after 1851, partly as a result of complaints of drunkenness and riotous behaviour.

When the Tunbridge Wells Races passed into history, the course was preserved as a footpath and bridle-way. It can still be followed today, apart from the section which crossed the Higher Cricket Ground, site of the winning post, stand, and enclosure. Betteridge's pictures show it in its modern aspect as a broad woodland ride. The trees, however, have mostly grown up within the last fifty years when the cessation of grazing allowed the limited deliberate plantings to seed themselves.

A child and her grandmother blackberrying along one of the complex network of footpaths on Tunbridge Wells Common. Brambles and bracken have flourished since grazing ceased, at the expense of the older heathland flora. In 1992 the Conservators adopted a management plan which aims to restore some heathland areas.This study, like the last, is one of a number in Betteridge's album depicting local residents enjoying the Commons.

'Two young monkeys' is the caption given by Harold Betteridge to this picture which he included in his section on the wildlife of the Commons! At this period (1962–4) and earlier, children used to roam all over the Commons, whose rocks, trees, and ponds provided ample scope for exploration. Nowadays only a few popular spots like Wellington Rocks and Denny Bottom serve a limited role as playgrounds.

Frederick Wadham Elers (right), mayor of Royal Tunbridge Wells in 1909–10, plants a scarlet chestnut on the Common on Saturday 30 December 1911, to commemorate the coronation of George V. The tree, supplied by nurseryman John Charlton to the order of an anonymous lady, was situated on open ground beside a footpath near the corner where Vale Road joins London Road. Today it is difficult to find, being surrounded by younger trees that have grown up over the intervening years.

'This charming heath remains in its natural beauty and verdure, a source of pleasure and of health to annually increasing multitudes', says Pelton's guide of 1874 in praise of Tunbridge Wells Common. 'In April and May the golden bloom of the furze, which is unusually profuse in this spot, delights the eye, and its rich perfume scents the breeze.'

This pair of panoramic views by George Glanville was reproduced in a souvenir album in 1896. The upper photograph is taken from Mount Ephraim, with Wellington Rocks and Victoria Grove to the left and the Higher Cricket Ground to the right. The other looks west from beside Major York's Road, with Fir Tree Pond in the right foreground.

Fonthill on the southern edge of Tunbridge Wells Common is said to be the site of the cottage of Mrs Humphreys, who gave Lord North a cup to drink from the chalybeate spring when he discovered it in 1606. She subsequently became the first dipper at the spring. The earliest town map (1738) shows a forge here. In 1833 the structures on the site were rebuilt in the form seen in this 1934 photograph by D.J. Johnson. On the left is Fonthill House, and on the right premises occupied by Arthur Aubin, farrier; Albert May, cabinet maker; and Norman and Goward, coach builder. The buildings were replaced by the present pavilion in 1939.

In 1858 William Law Pope, minister of King Charles' Church, instigated a scheme to provide work for the town's unemployed labourers, wages being paid by public subscription. The Freeholders' Committee gave permission for carrying out various works on Tunbridge Wells Common, including the creation of a 'greensward terrace walk' from near the end of the Pantiles to the Common's western boundary. The walk is in the foreground of this 1896 photograph by George Glanville. To the left is the Pump Room (built 1877–8).

The chalybeate spring from which Tunbridge Wells takes its name was discovered by Lord North on the edge of the Common. The first permanent structures here were erected by Thomas Neale, Lord of the Manor of Rusthall from 1682, after he had persuaded the Freeholders to accept an annual payment as compensation for loss of grazing rights. After a fire in 1687, he rebuilt the Pantiles in its present form. This view published by Harold Camburn about 1912 shows the bandstand erected in 1900.

York Cottage, probably built around 1800, is a survivor of several small dwellings on the Commons which were mostly replaced by more substantial structures in Victorian times. Like the road it stands on, it is named after Major Martin Yorke who served in the forces of the East India Company and took up residence in Bishops Down Grove (now the Spa Hotel) in 1772. This photograph (*c.* 1898) also shows the warehouse of William Rule, wine merchant and proprietor of the Swan Hotel.

The best-known work by William Pope's unemployed labourers in 1858 was Brighton Lake by Eridge Road, fed by a chalybeate spring on the northern bank. In 1897 an old resident recalled 'that most excellent man collecting the funds one very severe winter, and setting a great number of poor men to work in digging out what was then a bog'. Not everyone thought it was a good idea: others ridiculed it as a 'muddy ditch' and dubbed it 'Pope's Puddle' or 'Pope's Folly'.

An Edwardian postcard view of Fir Tree Pond, which was a well-known beauty spot around the turn of the century but subsequently fell into obscurity, reduced by the 1960s to a boggy hollow concealed by encroaching undergrowth. Situated beside Major York's Road, this was one of a number of informal ponds which were originally maintained as watering places for sheep and cattle. Along with Bracken Cottage Pond on the Common's western boundary, it was restored in 1992.

Fir Tree Pond was named after the two aged Scots pines, affectionately nicknamed Darby and Joan, which stood on top of the slope above and were encircled by a wooden bench. They were painted by a number of local artists in Victorian times. By the time of this photograph by Johnson Bird and Co. in the borough guide of 1902, one tree was clearly dying, and both had to be cut down in 1914. However, replacements were provided and can be seen on the site today.

The Spa Hotel was opened in 1878 as the Bishops Down Grove Spa and Hydropathic Sanatorium. It was an enlargement of a private house known as Bishops Down Grove, built in 1765 by Sir George Kelley, Sheriff of Kent, following his purchase of the Manor of Rusthall in 1758. His descendants have held the manor ever since, but the house was sold by Sir George's heirs to Major Yorke. This view by George Glanville was published in an album of his work in 1884.

'The famous Toad Rock is to Tunbridge Wells what the leaning tower is to Pisa', wrote E.V. Lucas in 1904. The Toad is the centre of a complex rockscape at Denny Bottom on Rusthall Common, first popularized for visitors in a guide of 1810. The many small dwellings clustering near the rocks preserve the area's original character as a settlement for quarrymen. George Glanville's photograph shows the Toad shortly before it was fenced in 1881–2 to prevent climbing.

The railings erected by the Freeholders were never very successful in keeping children off the Toad, as this (from around 1906) and many other old photographs bear witness. There was always a conflict between the area's role as a tourist attraction and as a playground for youngsters from the surrounding cottages. One Edwardian visitor, Charles Harper, was so irritated by the young locals as to declare in print that 'the population of Rusthall . . . must be in a very primitive stage of civilisation'.

Two ladies walking among the rocks at Denny Bottom about 1914. Martin and Row's town guide of *c*. 1907 reports that visitors to this spot were liable to be accosted by a self-appointed guide, who would emerge from one of the neighbouring cottages and offer a tour of the rocks, pointing out each one by name. 'From his lips you will learn that well nigh every rock has its name derived from a fancied resemblance to the things mentioned.'

A lantern slide of around 1880 looking down from Rusthall Road on Upper Street, Denny Bottom, with the Loaf Rock at the centre. The field in the left foreground was subsequently filled with more cottages. Some of the rocks in the area, like the Toad and the Loaf, have old established names, but it is clear that in Victorian times many others were freely invented for the benefit of visitors.

The Parson's Nose, or Pulpit Rock, resembling an enormous stone head looking out over Bull's Hollow, stands at the centre of this 1908 view taken from the footpath linking Rusthall Road and Harmony Street. Beside this footpath, though not in view here, is the Lion Rock, another early nineteenth-century discovery. It is not difficult to imagine the yarns that the local guides would have spun around these formations and others such as the Elephant, the Bloodstain, and the Footsteps.

The sandstone steps on the southern edge of Rusthall Common leading down into Happy Valley were probably constructed to provide the main access to the Cold Bath of 1708. Through the nineteenth century they gradually became buried and forgotten, but were subsequently rediscovered and feature prominently in Edwardian postcards and guidebooks, sometimes erroneously described as Roman. This picture by W.J. Rabson, stationer, of Vale Road, dates from about 1912.

St Paul's Church, Rusthall, seen here about 1905, was built in 1849–50 on the edge of the Common, a north aisle being added in 1864. The open area in the foreground, between the church and Langton Road, has since become heavily overgrown. The small pond, now vanished, is a remnant of an enormous marl pit shown on John Bowra's map of 1738. Two other marl pits do survive as ponds on the Common's north-west corner.

What postcard publisher Harold Camburn describes as the caves at Happy Valley are in fact no more than shallow excavations in the rocks to the west of the steps. Colbran's guide of 1839 describes them as 'dormitories for gipsies', but they were probably originally intended to shelter wooden seats and excavated at the time of the development of the Cold Bath to provide viewpoints over the valley.

The Cold Bath of 1708 lies just over the boundary of Rusthall Common in the grounds of the Beacon Hotel. It was originally covered by an ornamental pavilion and surrounded by pleasure grounds with lakes, watercourses, and fountains, but as early as 1766 it had fallen into disuse. Today most of the stonework is buried by mud and leaf-mould. This photograph published in the *Courier* shows it after excavation by Percy Nutting during the winter of 1947/8.

Southborough Common (seen here *c*. 1908) came into prominence in the 1880s when Southborough began to promote itself as a resort independent of Tunbridge Wells with its own attractions for visitors. A town guide of *c*. 1929 declares: 'That lover of beauty must be hard to please who does not admire the colony of oaks on the north, the pine tree temple on the west, the giant beeches . . . or the silver birches that cluster at the south-west. Flaring holly trees, grey-green juniper bushes and stretches of heather and bracken add variety of colouring in any weather. And to stand amid the golden glory of the gorse at Modest Corner is enough to cheer the most dismal of mortals.'

Clubs and Associations

The Tunbridge Wells Natural History and Philosophical Society had a pleasant outing to Heathfield on Saturday 24 June 1899. Led by George Abbott, seated fourth from left, the group examined the natural gas spring which was being used to light adjacent railway platforms and waiting rooms. After taking tea at the Cross in Hand Inn, the rest of the day was spent on the nearby downs. As one of its objectives, the society began a collection of natural history, geological, and ethnographical specimens and antiquities. Eventually this collection was adopted by the town council and it became the founding core of the holdings of the council's Tunbridge Wells Museum and Art Gallery.

Ten-year-old Wolf Cub Robert Hassell receives the Godfrey Phillips Shield from the Mayoress, Mrs J.A. McNab, on behalf of the St Andrew's Pack on 11 July 1953 in this *Courier* photograph. Sixteen packs had competed in the sports events, the St Andrew's Pack finishing with a three point lead over the runners-up, Pembury.

Sir Adrian and Lady Baillie entertained five hundred elderly people at their home, Leeds Castle, on 26 June 1939 as part of an outing organized by Tunbridge Wells Chamber of Trade. While welcoming his guests, Sir Adrian could not let the occasion pass without voicing thanks for the recent safe return of the King (George VI) and Queen from their tour of Canada and the United States. The old folk inspected the fortress and grounds before taking tea with the Baillies inside the castle.

The carriage of the Ancient Order of Druids (a friendly society) moves along the High Street during the George V coronation procession on 22 June 1911. A report in the *Advertiser* states that the float was 'lavishly decorated, and was covered with a canopy representing sky, with the sun, moon and stars depicted. In the car were the three Druidical Stones and four scrolls done in purple and gold, and on the sides of the car were the words, "Universal friendship, philanthropy and brotherly love," worked in red and blue on a white background.'

'Give with goodwill – give generously' was the slogan used by the Tunbridge Wells Rotary Club during the Goodwill appeal of 1953. In this *Advertiser* photograph the Mayor, Alderman J.A. McNab, is about to unveil the Goodwill Christmas tree outside the Great Hall at 11 a.m. on 5 December 1953. A second tree was unveiled on the Pantiles and collections were made house-to-house. The event was associated with the Rotary Club's appeal to assist the area's sick and elderly with meals for Christmas.

The 1955 Tunbridge Wells Fanciers' Show brought record numbers of entries from as far afield as Scotland. Entries totalled 641, of which 137 were rabbits. The prizes, awarded by Alderman J.A. McNab, were for every conceivable category of fancy rabbit and pigeon; from Netherland dwarfs to Himalayan adults and from 300 mile cocks to New Zealand Whites. Here, in a *Courier* photograph, the Mayor chats to society committee members before the presentations.

The British Legion's Tunbridge Wells branch held its annual children's party in the Crabb Hall in January 1954. The mayor, the vicar of Holy Trinity, and members of the legion were amongst the seventy-five guests. Mr and Mrs Taylor presented a threepenny piece to each child, and Mr W.V. Bradbury ran a film show after the 'bumper tea'. Balloons and presents were given to the children before they left.

The keeper of the royal philatelic collection, Sir John Wilson, was guest of honour at a luncheon at the Spa Hotel on 25 July 1953 in this *Courier* photograph. Stamp collectors from across the south-east had gathered for a coronation year philatelic rally. In his speech, Sir John posed the question, 'Will the increasing popularity of stamp collecting lead to the death of the hobby?', since so many ardent collectors were subsequently unwilling to part with their stamps.

An exhibition by the Tunbridge Wells Amateur Photographic Association held at the Technical Institute, where they leased a club room, in 1899. Their remarkable embroidered banner with its gold sun motif, presented by Lady Laura Salomons in 1895, is on prominent display. The society was founded in 1887, with Sir David Salomons, himself an enthusiastic photographer, as its patron. It changed its name to the Royal Tunbridge Wells Photographic Society in the 1950s.

Sir David Salomons (seated fifth from left) took an active interest in the Photographic Association. He regularly hosted outings to his residence at Broomhill, Southborough, and gave demonstrations of his pioneering electrical appliances and motor cars. On the occasion of this photograph by Percy Lankester in 1908, members of the Croydon Camera Club and the Eastbourne Photographic Society had been invited to participate. Joseph Chamberlain, Honorary Secretary of the Association from 1889 to 1909 is standing in the gap to Sir David's left. Hector Maclean, President of the Croydon Club, is behind the tripod at the right.

When the Victorian open air swimming pool in Grosvenor Recreation Ground was closed by the town council in 1948 as a danger to health and too expensive to renovate (it was filled in in 1954), there was considerable protest. The proprietors of the Woodsgate Country Club at Pembury offered to sell their pool (seen here *c.* 1950 and closed in 1973) to the council, but this was declined. The council's scheme to create a new pool at Dunorlan fell victim in 1953 to government restrictions on local authority spending.

The bowling green in Calverley Grounds was levelled in 1923 by unemployed labourers paid from the Mayor's Unemployment Fund; they also created a terrace on the park's north side. A pavilion for the green was supplied in 1924, and in 1926 the Calverley Grounds Bowling Club was formed. The tennis courts in the background on the right date from 1922. This photograph, by George King of Upper Grosvenor Road, was used in the official town guide from 1954.

A scene from the Tunbridge Wells Archery Tournament at the Nevill Ground in May 1938 by André Page of Southborough. The Tunbridge Wells Archery Club, formed around 1900 and surviving until the late 1950s, held frequent meetings at the ground in the summer. Local guides encouraged visitors to watch them in action: 'The spectacle of the green costumed "bowmen" (of both sexes) shooting their arrows at the vari-coloured targets is a most picturesque one.'

'Soccer interest runs high in Tunbridge Wells', says the 1937 town guide, 'for in addition to the local leagues . . . there is a professional side of long standing, the Tunbridge Wells Rangers, which enters teams in the Southern League and the Kent League as well as the English Cup and other similar competitions. Their ground is at Down Farm.' This photograph by H. Jenkins shows the Rangers shortly after adopting professionalism in 1904. The club was wound up in 1940 due to financial difficulties brought on by the war.

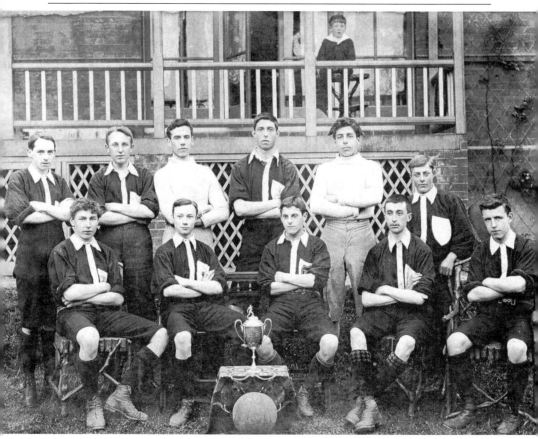

Woodbury Park Football Club, photographed here in 1898 by George Glanville, was one of the seventeen local teams which in 1899 formed the Tunbridge Wells and District Football League. They are displaying the Tunbridge Wells Boys Charity Cup which they won playing against the Robins before a crowd of 1,500 on the Lower Cricket Ground on 25 March 1898. The final of the Tunbridge Wells Charity Football Competition later in the year had 4,000 spectators. Both competitions raised money for local hospitals.

'Abe Mitchell, the famous professional (putting), taking part in a four-ball match. Mark Seymour and Albert Mitchell are seen on the left.' This scene on the Nevill Golf Course illustrates the 1927 town guide. The first nine holes were laid out before the First World War and the second nine afterwards. 'The land is eminently suited for golf, being sandy and quick drying, with natural hazards in the shape of gorse bushes. The greens are undulating and the approaches interesting and testing in the extreme.'

The Nevill Ground, seen here during County Cricket Week about 1907, was opened in 1898 by William Nevill, 1st Marquess of Abergavenny, from whom the land had been acquired by the Tunbridge Wells Cricket, Football and Athletic Club Ltd. A contemporary guide said that 'It deserves to be well patronised, for no expense was spared in making it perfect in every respect'. The first county cricket match on the ground was played in 1901, establishing a tradition that has continued to the present day.

F.E. Woolley's Kent XI and Tunbridge Wells and District XV on the occasion of their game on the Higher Cricket Ground on 28 April 1928 to raise funds for the proposed Kent and Sussex Hospital. The scores were Tunbridge Wells 213, Kent 121. Frank Woolley (Kent and England), seated fourth from left in the middle row, was a familiar figure at county matches on the Nevill Ground from 1906 to 1938, scoring ten centuries there. On his left is Alderman Charles Westbrook (mayor 1925–7 and 1938–45).

'In a country noted for its beautiful cricket grounds, the Nevill Ground in Tunbridge Wells possesses an unequalled charm and dignity; it has, in fact, frequently been described as the loveliest ground in England.' So writes the town guide contemporary with this photograph, taken on 29 June 1951, the last day of County Cricket Week, when Lancashire beat Kent by six wickets. When the ground opened, the Tunbridge Wells Cricket Club (1839) and the Blue Mantles (1864) transferred their headquarters there from the Common.

Buildings

A little south of Royal Tunbridge Wells, at Eridge, is the seat of the Marquesses of Abergavenny. Since the 1400s the Nevill family has occupied the site along with the castle of Abergavenny and its barony. Here they entertained Queen Elizabeth I in August 1573 during her progress through Kent and Sussex. However, the house decayed when the Nevills abandoned the place in the mid-1600s. The 2nd Earl of Abergavenny returned about 1789 and replaced most of the remnants of the house by this new mansion.

Gothic ornamentation was added to Eridge Castle, with heraldic plasterwork, turrets, castellated parapets, and mock-machicolations. Even the interior was decorated with a riot of heraldry, custom-made Gothic furniture, and stained glass windows depicting classical scenes. By 1938 the castle was said to be in decay, and, upon succeeding to the title, the 4th Marquess decided to demolish the building entirely and to erect the existing more modern and convenient dwelling.

The Pantiles viewed from the south end on a winter's day at the turn of the century. At the north end is Bath House and the chalybeate spring. Dr Lodwick Rowzee, in his treatise *The Queens Welles* of 1656, described the numerous ailments for which the Tunbridge water was considered to be a successful cure – the water 'doth effectually open all manner of Obstructions, wheresoever they be lurking'. Later, he insists that it 'is good against the gravel & the stone in the kidneys . . . it is good also for all inward ulcers . . . dropsie, the black & yeallow jaundise, the *Schirrus Lienis*, or hard swelling of the spleen . . . all inveterate Dysenteries or bloudy Flixes: as also all other Fluxes of the belly . . . it driveth away besides all manner of wormes . . . it may be used also for the Gout', and, in conclusion, he informs women that there is nothing better to make them fruitful.

The Bath House, erected by Lady of the Manor Elizabeth Shorey in 1803–5, was never a great success. After some years of virtual disuse, it was shut down in 1847. The building was taken over by John Luck, dealer in glass and porcelain, whose souvenir china with black transfer printed local views is still familiar to collectors. The business was carried on by his widow and son until 1902. Boots Cash Chemists, seen in this view by D.J. Johnson, acquired the premises in 1904/5.

Local postcard publisher Harold Camburn's view from around 1910 of the terrace of cottages in Little Mount Sion variously known as Sion Crescent and Queen Anne's Mansion (from the local legend that the Queen stayed here). They originated as two of the town's early lodging houses, built by Philip Seale in 1689 and 1694, but by the nineteenth century had been subdivided into small tenements. Having fallen into disrepair, they were demolished in 1913. The Toc H hall now stands on the site.

The lower end of the High Street, photographed *c.* 1907. Premises of note include, to the far right, at no. 81 the establishment of H. Seymour Cousens, photographer, who employed natural light via a glass roof to his first floor studio. Also visible are the shops of Allen Parsons, coal merchant, and John Harrington, confectioner. On the far left, next to William Moor, bootmaker, is the shop of Lancaster and Cunningham, furnishers and removers, whose sign 'To & From All Parts' shows an oriental scene with an Indian elephant pulling one of their pantechnicons.

The Castle Hotel in London Road, not to be confused with the long-vanished seventeenth-century Castle Tavern on Mount Ephraim, was built around 1800 when Castle Street (originally New Street) was created. Renamed as the Castle about 1815, it was rebuilt in its present form by proprietor William Urquhart in 1896. It ceased to be a hotel in the 1970s. This view was published by Harold Camburn about 1920.

Vale Towers, photographed here by D.J. Johnson in 1934, was built in the 1830s as Romanoff House, Thomas Allfree's 'classical school for the education of young gentlemen'. Allfree had been tutor to the Russian royal family. In the 1860s the school moved to Rose Hill next door (the entrance is seen here on the left) and changed its name accordingly. In the mid-1960s Rose Hill School moved to Culverden Down. Note the delivery boy's cycle belonging to butcher R.A. Ashby.

Mount Pleasant, seen here about 1890, originated as a country lane linking the old town centred on the Pantiles and Mount Sion with John Ward's new town designed by Decimus Burton on the Calverley Estate in the late 1820s and 1830s. As late as 1874, Pelton's guide could still tell visitors that 'Mount Pleasant, a sylvan avenue leading northward from the railway station, amply justifies its name'. In this view the bay windowed shop of R.W. Weekes, draper and undertaker, appears next to the single storied Bridge Tavern and more Weekes premises. The terrace of shops further up the hill was constructed in the 1870s, but the opposite side was not developed until the 1930s.

On these two pages are four comparable views of the development of the bottom of Mount Pleasant. This first photograph, of the 1860s, shows the original buildings. To the left of Alfred Drake's Railway Bell public house, on the corner, are the modest premises of outfitter R.W. Weekes, J. Pearce (stationer and Tunbridge ware repository), and John Apps's Bridge Tavern.

By the time of this view, at the turn of the century, the Railway Bell had hardly changed. But, evidently, the Weekes business had prospered. Weekes had erected matching buildings on each side of the Railway Bell. Likewise, the former Bridge Tavern had elevated itself to an hotel of four storeys with turrets. The railway bridge (foreground) of 1851 survived, although it was increasingly considered as a bottleneck and eyesore.

Plans to improve the railway bridge were suggested and postponed in 1878 but at last approved in 1903. Beginning in 1906 the bridge was replaced by one much wider which was opened by the Mayor on 16 May 1907, shortly before this photograph was made. Most of the supporting structure was erected by the railway company, the two main girders being 10 feet high and 108 feet and 68 feet long with a total weight of supporting steel of 461 tons. The corporation was responsible for the kerbing, paving, and decorative features.

This photograph was taken soon after the completion of Blomfield's 1912 new downside railway station building. The Railway Bell Hotel had been demolished in 1911 and replaced by a grand extension to Weekes, built to match the buildings existing on either side. Weekes still owned premises beyond the Bridge Hotel which did not link to the corner building until after the hotel closed down in 1937.

Grove Hill Road seen from the foot of Mount Pleasant in 1911. The offices, opened in 1897, of the *Tunbridge Wells Advertiser* (founded in 1880), decorated for the coronation of George V, are on the corner to the right. On the other side of the road a sign on the skyline marks the premises of the town's rival paper, the *Kent and Sussex Courier*, first published in 1872. Next door to the *Courier* office were the premises of Harold Camburn, who published this view as a postcard.

Rusthall High Street, *c.* 1905. On the far right is the Rusthall Congregational Church, which was built by Messrs Wilson and Finch in 1861 and enlarged in 1907. Beyond the church at this time were the premises of J.E. Rumens (The People's Stores), then a watchmaker, a stationer, an outfitter, a tobacconist, a dining room, a harness maker, a grocers, and a post office. Opposite were The Morning Star public house (not visible), a baker, a fishmonger, a pork butcher, a dairyman, and a general butcher.

Chancellor House, Mount Ephraim, as photographed by D'Ath and Condon, was situated in grounds behind The Chalet, Thomas Barton's Tunbridge ware manufactory. The house was built about 1676 by Judge Jefferies, although it is said that he never actually lived in the town. There were several royal or noble residents. Queen Amelié lived here in the mid-1800s, and in 1932 Queen Mary visited her former lady-in-waiting Lady Hillingdon at the house. The house was demolished to make way for flats, c. 1939.

London Road at the turn of the century. To the left are the rocks atop which stands St Helena cottage. Now-buried caves excavated for sand at the base of the rocks were lost when the road was regraded by the Turnpike Trustees in 1833. The caves were reopened briefly for use as air raid shelters during the Second World War. On the horizon is the tower and spire of Emmanuel Church (1867–1974) which replaced the original chapel of the Countess of Huntingdon's Connexion.

André Page's photograph of Parham House, at the junction of Church and Mount Pleasant Roads. Private plans in 1934 to demolish Parham House and to replace it with a 'super-cinema' momentarily postponed plans for a civic assembly hall. The possibilities were discussed of the new cinema doubling as a venue for civic and public events, thus avoiding the expense of an assembly hall. However, the council opted for a venue owned by itself, constructed to its own specifications.

Church Road, photographed by S.K. Lazell. The Ritz Buildings, dominated by the cinema, opened in 1934. The cinema name changed several times, for many years from 1954 being the Essoldo, and most recently becoming the MGM cinema. Here the Essoldo features the 1960 Claude Rains film *The Lost World*. Further along Church Road the skyline has not yet been ruptured by the blocks of Europa House (on the left between nos 5 and 11) and Telephone House (on the right between nos 8 and 16).

Crescent Road photographed before 1915. The properties on the left were demolished after the first Crescent Road car park had been opened in 1957. In 1908 these were the premises of G.B. Donovan, a cabinet maker, at no. 22; Saunders Bros. Ltd, stationers, at no. 23; and the Victoria Tavern, a Kenward Court Ltd brewery public house, of 2 High Street, at no. 24. The shop then occupied by George Burnell and Son, upholsterers, general house fitters, and undertakers, at no. 25, and those beyond up to no. 29 survived until 1961. A much larger multi-storey car park was begun in 1967 and was opened on 2 October 1968.

Demolition work at Calverley Parade for the proposed new civic centre begins in
October 1931. The Parade had been acquired for a civic centre as early as 1895,
although many delays followed. Work did not begin until after a political storm in the
early 1930s. In August 1930 the town council endorsed the civic centre scheme. But, in
1931 the Burgesses Emergency Committee resolved to contest, at the November
election, the re-election of any councillor who voted for the new municipal buildings.

The town hall site cleared and ready for building in June 1937. The 1931 election
resulted in the Ratepayers' and Burgesses' Association sweeping the board; six
councillors losing their seats to association candidates. Once the parade site was largely
clear, arguments continued over the best usage. Since a new purpose-built civic centre
was not imminent, in July 1932 the Special (Calverley Parade Property) Committee
suggested that at least all council departments could be drawn together physically by
utilizing the Calverley Terrace properties.

Despite the 1932 municipal elections upset, by April 1933 the new civic centre plans were receiving encouragement from the Chamber of Trade and growing public support. By 1937 most of the council offices had moved to Calverley Terrace, and erection of the civic centre was underway. In this *Advertiser* view the last part of Calverley Parade is seen being demolished as late as April 1939. Numbers nine and ten Calverley Terrace were to be retained pending use of the site for a new fire station, but the semi-detached pair survived.

Sydney Lazell's view of the completed civic centre. Fifty years after the project was conceived, the largest part of the new complex, the town hall, was opened on 20 March 1941 by the Mayor, Alderman C.E. Westbrook. By that time the £29,126 police station and court and the £59,240 Assembly Hall had both been opened to the public. The £19,765 library and museum building was complete but bare internally, and the £72,850 town hall was complete as far as the exigencies of war would allow.

Lazell's view of the Assembly Hall's interior. Opened on 24 May 1939, the hall included some of the latest innovations in theatre equipment. Amongst the luxurious features, a contemporary *Advertiser* account listed 'washed, purified, continually changed and heated air . . . a floor that can be either "sprung" for dancing or "locked" for other occasions . . . provision for thirty lines of scenery . . . groups of Portland stone depicting dancing, drama and music . . . Travertine marble . . . and . . . below the stage are the boiler and machine rooms, which should make remarkably good air-raid shelters, for they had to be excavated out of sandstone.'

St Augustine's Roman Catholic Church, Grosvenor Road. The church was built in a classical style of local sandstone to a design by Joseph Ireland. The imposing bell tower came in 1889, designed by B.A. Elphicke. Closed in 1967, the building was demolished in 1968 to make room for a supermarket. A new St Augustine's was opened in Crescent Road in 1975.

Harold Page's photograph of the Salvation Army Citadel in Varney Street. Built in 1886, it was a curious red brick romanesque building with stone classical ornaments, pediments, and volutes. It was succeeded in 1970 by a new Citadel in Bayhall Road. The site of Varney Street, like several minor streets north of Calverley Road, is now occupied by the Royal Victoria Place shopping development.

The Baptist Tabernacle in Calverley Road was opened on New Year's Day 1884. Members of the Baptist community broke away from the existing churches in 1873 over the issue of open communion. Subsequently the new congregation met mainly at the town hall, with Revd W.K. Armstrong as pastor, until in September 1881 a resolution was made to pursue a purpose-built building. The architects were Messrs Lander and Bedells, and the building was erected by Samuel Woods of Weybridge.

The first deacons of the baptist tabernacle were, standing, A.T. Reeve, J. Botten, G. Finch, P. Dodd, J. Capell, and R.J. Pennington, and seated, D. Cavie, Revd J. Smith (pastor), and T. Young. The church was built at a cost of £5,782 12s 6d and a schoolroom was added in 1892. The building of the two was largely credited to the zeal of Revd Smith who was 'called to Higher Service' in 1897. In 1938 the tabernacle was succeeded by one in Upper Grosvenor Road.

Camden Road, seen here around 1908, began as a track leading from the Calverley Estate to the waterworks which supplied the new development and the quarry from which the building stone was taken. It was developed as a shopping street in the 1850s. In the right foreground of this view is Mrs R. Carr's shop for ladies' and children's clothing, and, further up, the overhanging signs mark the premises of H.A. Busse and Company, antique and general furniture dealers; Albert Baynes, confectioner and toy merchant; and Lewarn Clayton, draper and ladies' outfitter. On the left can be seen Walton Brothers' butchers shop, Taylor's dining rooms, and Ernest King's pianoforte, organ, and music warehouse.

Camden Road Methodist Church, from a lantern slide. The first Primitive Methodist services were held on the Common, eventually transferring to Mount Sion Chapel. The Camden Road building replaced an earlier church on the site, erected in 1856–7. The second church was built to Renaissance-style designs by Weeks and Hughes in 1877–8 for almost £4,000, and it was opened in 1878 by Revd Dr Antliff. Another church of brick with Bath stone dressings, internally it had a gallery on ornate iron columns. Following a final service on 30 August 1981 the building was sold for use as an antiques saleroom. The church was situated between 124 and 126 Camden Road and is now the site of a recently completed shops and flats development.

George Glanville's *c.* 1899 photograph of the newly finished St Barnabas Church in Stanley Road. Costing £17,970 *2s 6d* the church was built to a Gothic style in red brick with sandstone dressings to a design by J.E.K. and J.P. Cutts. Building began in 1887, and the church was consecrated on 18 May 1893. The Cutts plans included a tower and spire, though these were omitted subsequently. In 1992 an attractive shingled flèche atop the roof was removed.

Bayhall, Pembury, *c.* 1915, when known as 'The Haunted House'. The mansion was largely rebuilt by Richard Amherst, whose father had bought the property from the Earl of Dorset in the early 1600s. The building was completed in about 1664. By the early 1700s the building was a substantial mansion surrounded by hanging gardens, fish ponds, ornamental walks, and farm buildings. However, during the 1800s the building gradually fell into decay, and, except for a couple of wall fragments, has now all but vanished.

Until its demolition in 1928, Great Culverden house stood on what became the site of the Kent and Sussex Hospital. The house was built in 1829–30 for J. Jeddere Fisher to a design by Decimus Burton. It was said to enjoy 'all the domestic comforts, and even luxuries, appertaining to an English gentleman's home.' On the extensive Culverden estate Fisher also erected Swiss Cottage, partly hewn out of sandstone, and Culverden Castle.

St John's Road about 1908, looking towards St John's Church on the left. The church was opened in 1858 and extensively altered and enlarged in 1896. In the left foreground are the premises of Leonard Scott, coal, coke, wood, corn, hay, straw, and seed merchant, and the Red Lion public house (of *c*. 1850). The ivy-clad building further up is St John's School, established *c*. 1860. On the right is Thomas Warrener's North Ward Stores. A sign on the skyline indicates the A1 Furnishing Company.

St Luke's Church, St Luke's Road, was built in 1910 to designs by Egbert Cronk. Constructed of ragstone and Bath stone, and designed to seat 500 people, the building cost £7,500. Miss Adelaide Anne Mitchell donated £1,500 towards the new church, whilst later she bought land for the church on Wilkin Road and paid for the tower and bell as a memorial to her parents. On 26 February 1910 Miss Mitchell laid the foundation stone, and only eight months later, 31 October, the Bishop of Rochester consecrated the church. In 1924 the parish gave three stained glass windows in memory of Miss Mitchell.

S.K. Lazell's photograph of the Christian Scientist Church in St John's Road before it was transformed in 1959 to offices for Hospital Service Plan (later named Private Patients Plan). The church was built in 1931 to designs by Cecil Burns which employed an exposed concrete frame, an open arcade along the front, and attractive concrete tracery in the two main windows headed by segmental arches. Now the arcade is lost along with the tracery. Having been taken over by the Freight Transport Association, the building was re-opened as Hermes House by the Minister of Transport on 25 November 1975, and Sir Patrick Mayhew opened an imposing extension to the building on 10 July 1987.

The northern end of St John's Road, at the junction with Powder Mill Lane (named after a gunpowder works established in 1771), around 1906. On the right is the Cross Keys Inn, dating from *c.* 1800. Of the cottages beyond, on the site now occupied by the inn's car park, one was destroyed by a gale in 1925 and the remainder were pulled down in the 1930s. The terrace opposite was demolished in the 1950s to make way for the new Technical High School for Boys.

Southborough, although an older settlement than Tunbridge Wells and one that provided lodgings for the earliest visitors to the chalybeate spring in the seventeenth century, did not develop into a town until the late nineteenth century. It acquired its first local government in 1894, when an urban district council was established. This view of the Parade, London Road, looking north from the junction with Vale Road, is from an album of Southborough views published by stationer Richard Fielder about 1897.

This view of the northern end of London Road, Southborough, taken by Tunbridge Wells photographer Henry Inskipp about 1870, shows the apex of the Common before the arrival of the now familiar lamp-surmounted fountain erected by the inhabitants in 1886 to the memory of local doctor William Fairlie Clarke. The freehold of Southborough Common was purchased by the urban district council in 1948. In the distance on the right is the Hand and Sceptre Hotel, said to date from the late seventeenth century and remodelled into its present form in 1897.

E. Paget Thurstan's book *Southborough . . . its Attractions as a Health Resort*, published in 1885 to promote the town as a rival to its larger neighbour, relates how 'Sir William Gull (the well-known physician), stood on Southborough Common and said "It is impossible in any part of the world to breathe purer air."' 'A portion of Southborough Common', he writes, 'is open grassland, but more than half is well wooded, and contains here exquisite little fairy dells, there stately colonnades of trees, and isolated monarchs of the forest'. One noted beauty spot on the edge of the Common was Holden Corner Pond, pictured here in another view by Henry Inskipp.

The Church of St Thomas, Pennington Road, Southborough, is seen here in its original state. In 1860–1 it was built at the expense of Mrs Sarah Pugh because she was dissatisfied with the Low Church character of Southborough's parish church, St Peter's. The building was constructed in ragstone with Bath stone dressings to a Decorated design by H. Pownall. The church has had several alterations. A south transept was added in 1888 by R.H. Garling. Other changes include enlarged south and north aisles, a west porch, and an apse at the west end of the southern aisle. In the Lady Chapel hangs an attractive copy of Sandro Botticelli's tondo *Our Lady of the Magnificat* which was given in 1923.

Bibliography

Some of these works are out of print. However, they should be available through libraries. Works already listed in the first volume of old photographs are omitted from this list.

Anon. N.d. *Picturesque Tunbridge Wells*. Dundee: J. Valentine & Sons Ltd.

Anon. N.d. *Southborough*. R. Fielder.

Anon. [Coster, T., and F. Roberts]. N.d. *The 'High Rocks' Hotel and Pleasure Grounds*. Tunbridge Wells: Henry Gardner.

Anon. 23 October 1895. 'Carriages without Horses. A Chat with Sir David Salomons'. *The Sketch* XI: 699–702.

Anon.*c.* 1899. *Pictures of Tunbridge Wells and Neighbourhood*. Tunbridge Wells: L. Hepworth & Co. Ltd.

Anon. *c.* 1929. *The Official Guide to Southborough*. Cheltenham: E.J. Burrow & Co. Ltd.

Anon. 1934. *Baptist Tabernacle, Tunbridge Wells – Souvenir Programme of Jubilee Celebrations*. Tunbridge Wells: Baptist Tabernacle.

Anon. 1934. *Souvenir of the New Kent and Sussex Hospital*. Tunbridge Wells: John Jarvis Ltd.

Anon. [Cowan, C.]. 1964. *A Descriptive Guide and Souvenir of The High Rocks*. Tunbridge Wells: Stanford Printing Company.

Antell, J. Autumn 1993. 'A Great Victorian Nurseryman'. *Royal Tunbridge Wells Civic Society Newsletter*.

Clifford, J. 1829. *The Visitor's Guide to Tunbridge Wells containing an Account of the Ancient and present State of that Place, with Rules for Drinking the Waters*. Tunbridge Wells: J. Clifford.

Copus, G. 1967. *The Early History of St. Barnabas' Parish, Tunbridge Wells*. Tunbridge Wells: G. Copus.

Copus, G. 1987. *St Barnabas' Tunbridge Wells – A Miscellany*. Tunbridge Wells: G. Copus.

Curteis, Mrs R.M., and Lady Hawley. 1930. 'Bayhall, Pembury'. *Archaeologia Cantiana* 42:173–6.

Goffin, R. 1990. *Harry Pratley – A Bookseller Remembers*. Westerham: Hurtwood Press Ltd.

Gunnis, R. N.d. *Eridge Castle and the Family of Nevill*.

Harper, C.G. 1906. *The Hastings Road*. London: Chapman and Hall Ltd.

Lucas, E.V. 1904. *Highways and Byways in Sussex*. London: MacMillan.

Mathieson. 1867. *Mathieson's Tunbridge Wells and Tunbridge (Including Southborough, Frant, & Pembury) Directory*. Tunbridge Wells: R. Pelton.

Parkes, J. N.d. *The Story of Three David Salomons at Broomhill*. Privately published.

Squirrell, F.C. 1945. *Civic Defence – A History of Civil Defence in the Borough of Royal Tunbridge Wells 1939–45*. Tunbridge Wells: Courier Co. Ltd.

Tapsell, M. 1987. *Memories of Kent Cinemas*. Croydon: Plateway Press.

Thurstan, E.P. 1885. *Southborough its Chalybeate Springs, Climate, and Attractions as a Health Resort*. Tunbridge Wells: The Courier Printing and Publishing Company.

Acknowledgements

We are grateful to the following people for assistance during the research of this book: M.M. Brant, M. Goulden, N. Hill, G.W. Pentecost, and M.B. Streeten. For permission to reproduce photographs we thank: Courier Printing and Publishing Co. Ltd, D. Fletcher of the Tank Museum, R.J. Glass, B. Lazell, H. Page, and M. Page.